For

Pauline

(PMW)

14/2/16

Sin, Sex and Psychology

THE CATHOLIC CHURCH ON THE COUCH

P. M. Webb

ISBN: 1514669021

ISBN 13: 9781514669020

A THERAPEUTIC APPROACH TO THE MANY PROBLEMS

FACING THE CATHOLIC CHURCH TODAY, USING

THE METHODS OF SIGMUND FREUD, INSTEAD OF

PHILOSOPHY.

www. catholicchurchonthecouch

For Jo Sullivan.

Many thanks to Rosemarie Langley without whose help and support in every possible way, this book would probably never have seen the light of day.

Many thanks also to Monica Hutchinson for her personal help in so many ways and to Dr. William Makin for many discussions and corrections of fact. Thanks also to Mary Donaghey for constantly keeping the show on the road.

Contents

P. M. Webb

Introduction

The times are out of joint.

Shakespeare

The Catholic Church, which has flourished in Europe for two thousand years, now seems to be dying in Europe and the West. It is increasingly obvious that in very many places, the Church is in freefall crisis. However, most ordinary Catholics passionately want the Church to survive, it is an important part of our lives, and we have lived by it. It is ours.

There is no doubt that the Church, in what we call the developed world, seems to be really sick. Parish numbers have dropped dramatically and there are fewer priests. Most of the priests belong to the "grey haired brigade" as a friend of mine calls them.

In the diocese in which I live, our bishop has told us that seven elderly priests in this diocese are due to retire this year, and there are not enough young priests to replace them. Since then, three more priests have died, one of them comparatively young. There are a few young priests, but not nearly enough to replace the others, so parishes will have to be merged and communities broken up. If it were not for a number of ex-Anglican priests, married men and now Catholic priests, the situation would be even more dire than it is.

Congregations are elderly. Many of my friends, good Catholics all their lives, have middle aged children who, in spite of a "good Catholic education", are no longer interested in organised religion, and who no longer go to Mass - the one sign of a practising Catholic. Frequently, grandchildren are not baptised.

There are many questions which need to be asked and some answers are urgently required.

Why do Catholics no longer go to regular confession in large numbers as they used to?

Why has there been so much child abuse by clergy?

Why are there so few priests?

Why do children of "good Catholic parents" no longer go to Mass? And why are *their* children not baptised?

By what strange, bizarre logic does the Church strip the priesthood from Catholic priests who want to get married, and yet welcome married ex-Anglican clergy with open arms?

Why does the church refuse to accept the necessity for birth control?

Why are divorced Catholics refused Communion?

The Church frequently quotes the teaching of the "Natural Law" in sexual matters. What is the "Natural Law"? Is it the same as the Law of Nature?

What on earth is going on? Why is this happening? Why do the ancient certainties suddenly seem not certain at all?

Some Catholics blame the Catholic schools and say that the faith is not being taught in the way that it used to be, and children no longer have to learn the catechism off by heart. Others blame the Second Vatican Council of the church. Since then they say, everything has begun to fall apart. Vatican II, they believe, was dominated by liberals, hardly Catholics at all, whose influence has been catastrophic.

As a result of Vatican II some are bitter that the liturgy of the church is no longer in Latin, so that the liturgy is no longer universal in the way that it used to be.

Others blame the pressures of modern living and the relentless sexualisation of society. The startling headlines of the past announced that a priest had a secret woman or a child. The headlines of the last few years have been much darker, with the revelations of sexual abuse of children, and the resulting cover-ups.

I would like to suggest something much simpler and more fundamental than any of these. Over the centuries it has often been said by theologians that "Philosophy is the handmaid of Theology". A handmaid is a servant or slave. This means that philosophy, the logic, reason and ordered thinking of the ancient Greeks, long before the birth of Jesus, is of immense importance in Christian teaching. However, like many elderly servants, Philosophy seems to have taken over rather too much of the household management.

The assistance of a much younger, more dynamic handmaid, called Psychology, might be of greater use to the Church and help us to see what the real problems are. Therapy always goes back to the very beginnings of things. That is my main aim throughout this book.

Chapter One

A Strange Apology

"Philosophy is the handmaid of theology"

Attributed to St. John of Damascus   7th century

In the year 2,000, Pope John Paul II did a very strange thing; he made an apology to a man who had been dead for hundreds of years. The man in question was, of course, Galileo. Four hundred years earlier, Galileo had been tried in a Church court and found guilty of heresy. The heresy in question was that the earth, instead of remaining quietly and steadily in one place for ever, with the sun and moon going round it by day and night, was in fact hurtling around the sun at incredible speeds, and not only that, but spinning like a top while it did so. The Church had accepted this as a thesis, an idea, for some time, but the minute Galileo insisted that it was really, literally true he was in trouble.

Many people didn't like it at the time. Given the difficulties we have in accepting the new idea of global warming, you can see that the notion of a high speed, spinning earth wasn't a comfortable thought. Up till that moment, the received wisdom for most people was that the earth stayed sensibly in one place and the sun went round the earth every twenty-four hours.

The moon kept changing shape all the time and occasionally disap-pearing altogether. In the really ancient world, before Christianity, many people thought that the moon was a goddess and what did you expect, because women have menstrual cycles and are notorious for changing their minds anyway.

However the Church was very definite about the earth staying in one place and the sun going round it. It fitted the neat mathematical model of the philosophers who were most admired by theologians. In the early seventeenth century, after the Reformation, the Church was all in favour of stability. Flighty nonsense about planets zooming around the universe was not, it thought, what the faithful required at the time.

Now, as a great scientist, Galileo was a sensible man, and didn't really want trouble, so he agreed that he was wrong, the earth didn't move, and he even signed a document saying that he was wrong. But there is a story that as he left the court for a life of house imprisonment, he was heard to mutter under his breath "Puor si muove", meaning "Of course it moves."

So why is this important now? For the simple reason that exactly the same thing happened in the twentieth century. The Church has ignored one of the great original thinkers of the time. That man is the Austrian Jew, Sigmund Freud, and his discovery of psychoanalysis.

The Church is not the only institution to ignore new ideas and find them unwelcome. It happens all the time, often with governments, but because of the Church's emotional power over millions of people, this can have far-reaching results for everyone.

SIGMUND FREUD

We have in Freud a man whose effect on the world, whether we like it or not, is every bit as influential as Galileo was in his day. In the same way that Galileo has changed the way we looked at the earth, the moon and the sun, Freud has totally changed the way in which we think about people and why they behave in the ways that they do. As Freud was an atheist Jew living in Austria, the Church ignored him, as if he had never existed, and still does.

A friend of mine once told a priest that he had a crazy friend who thought that the Church needed Freud. The priest in question, a kindly man, laughed gently and said, "Oh, I think we can do without Freud." However, in the following two weeks after that comment, even I was shocked to read newspaper articles, not only about abusing priests, but also about a much-respected Belgian bishop, abusing his nephew, and the cover-ups of abuse by Cardinal Law in Boston. The lurid newspaper stories used to be about priests with mistresses, or children, but we have moved on since then.

Either we think of these abusing men as evil, totally perverted sinners, or we think that something has gone horribly wrong. If something has gone horribly wrong, then it needs to be put right.

A clearer understanding of what sexuality means to people, is exactly what the Church *does* need at this time - but Freud! Isn't he the one responsible for all this sexual revolution and general carryings on? Isn't it his fault that society is crumbling and no one has any morals any more? The Church has been so terrified by his talk of sexuality that it did not, and still does not, want to know. All the other Churches seem to feel the same. However, a growing army of counsellors and therapists who came after Freud want us to look deep within ourselves, to see what makes us tick.

FREUD AND THE SOUL

Freud did not talk about "the mind", though most English and American people think that he did, because that's how Freud's work was translated from German into English. But although he described himself as "as unbelieving Jew," an atheist, the German word he actually used was not "mind", but *soul.*

3

Now the Catholic Church has for thousands of years considered itself to be the great expert on people's souls. What could Freud, "the unbelieving Jew", possibly have to say about souls, that the Church did not already know? Fortunately for us, however, he *was* an atheist "unbelieving Jew", because if he had been a Catholic, he would never have dared to think as he did.

There is a split in the Church. The mind of the intellectual, orthodox, institutional Catholic Church, as opposed to its heart, seems often to have thought of souls *from the outside*, logically and rationally. Looked at in this way, souls are *things* about which you can make statements, good, bad, disordered, damned or saved. In the intellectual world you can think about people and situations as being ideal, in the nitty gritty of reality, they never are. We need to look at souls from the *inside*, and ask "what is going on?"

Freud's early clients were very often emotionally ill, hysterical middle class men or women, with very strange ways of behaving. They were often sent to him by fathers or husbands who wanted to know if the women could be helped.

Gradually, Freud discovered that his clients, male or female, did not want him to tell them what was wrong with them, they often knew what was wrong with them, and they wanted to talk about it. Eventually he developed a method where clients lay on a couch for about an hour and talked, and he sat behind them, listening, and making occasional comments. His theories are based on what they told him, and the intensive study he made of his own behaviour and feelings, and those of his friends and colleagues.

What the women who were his patients frequently said was, that they had been sexually abused as children and young women, and this had seriously affected their behaviour as adults.

At the time, at the end of the nineteenth century, this was seen by most men, including doctors and clergymen, as twisted lying or insane delusions, which proved that these women were totally mad and ought to be locked up. However, Freud realised that they weren't lying. He tried to tell people this in writing and lectures to doctors and medical men. Such was the enormous opposition that he was unable to continue and began to doubt himself.

Still believing that his clients were sane and serious, he began to wonder if perhaps there was an element of fantasy in all this. If it was fantasy he needed to know why, and so developed his theory of the Oedipus complex.

The theory of the Oedipus complex tells us much about the basic relationships between parents and children, it is very powerful and helps us to understand the way families work. However, he should have stayed with the original truth. Many feminists, especially in the USA have blamed him bitterly for not doing so, but well over a hundred years ago in the authoritarian society of Vienna, it was probably impossible.

WHAT IS THE HUMAN SOUL?

When I was a young teacher, it was my job to teach Catholic religion to a class of eleven-year-old children. One of the chapters in the officially approved book I was using, tried to show the meaning of the word "soul" by a little picture, which the teacher was to draw on the blackboard. It consisted of an outline of a human being (definitely sexless) drawn with a firm line, and beneath this was written "the body". Next to it was an identical drawing but this time drawn with a broken, dotted line, so that it looked insubstantial, and beneath this was written, "The soul".

I was supposed to explain that this dotted figure was the spirit, which lived in the body, but was not the same thing. Even then, I knew that as a description of spirit, it left much to be desired, and explained nothing. It certainly didn't explain anything to me, but I was at a loss to know how to think about this in any other way.

There was no idea that this ghostly, dotted, human outline on the blackboard called "the soul", was connected in any way with the thoughts, feelings, needs and desires of my human heart and body, or the thoughts, feelings, needs and desires of the children in front of me. In fact, if they did have thoughts, feelings or desires, they should forget about them, and concentrate on the lesson.

The soul, in this way of thinking, is a totally separate, abstract, intellectual, cut-off thing, a part of me that I cannot reach. The soul was presented as a philosophical concept, rather than a human reality. However, Jesus said, "the Kingdom of Heaven is within you" - our souls are within us, and they do consist of our thoughts, feelings and desires, and this is psychology.

There is a deep split here - I think that many Catholics looked at the soul from the inside too, but it wasn't considered theological. The spiritual side of religion, mysticism the love of mankind, generosity, kindness compassion, contemplative prayer, trust in God, meditation, the deep study of the inside of humanity, was split off, put to one side, and labelled "devotional". This was not the serious intellectual business of serious, intellectual rational theologians, who used philosophy, reason and logic to understand about God

The care for the poor, the compassion for struggling humanity, was often accomplished by holy people such as St. Benedict, Mother Julian of Norwich, Francis of Assisi, and in our own time by Mother Theresa. Calling them "Saints" somehow puts them outside the reach of ordinary people, as if they are not for public imitation. There used to be a Catholic joke that you could go to Hell trying to imitate the saints, but the really, really important thing was what you believed intellectually.

Four hundred years ago, Saint Teresa of Avila, a Spanish woman, wrote a great book entitled "The Interior Castle" referring to the exploration of the castle of her soul, her mind, based entirely on her own prayer, self-analysis, and spiritual experience, her psychology. This book has always been regarded by the Church as "mystical" and therefore of little consequence for theology which is based on reason.

As a result, the Church's official descriptions of the soul, "pure, sinful, consecrated, good, bad, lost", often seemed to be from the outside, and sometimes seemed to be a theoretical idea, very little to do with what Jesus described as "The kingdom of God within you".

The reason for this is that *thinking about* the soul, as opposed to praying or meditating, is based on logic and reason, which is a way of thinking inherited from the pagan philosopher Aristotle, brought into the Church over seven hundred years ago ago by St. Thomas Aquinas.

Now, Freud, as a doctor, knew that there was something wrong with people. In fact you don't have to be clever, or modern, everybody has always known that there is something wrong with people. We have all sorts of odd ways of behaving, and sometimes very bad ways.

However, looking at the soul in the way Jesus did, as the centre of our being, psychology insists that the way we can know about our own soul, as adults, is not by philosophical reasoning, but by looking inside ourselves, looking at our feelings.

This means the exploration of what we think, feel and desire, or have thought and felt since childhood. If we have really serious psychological

7

problems, this should preferably be done with someone who has been trained to the work. We have to think about ourselves, and our difficulties.

THE KINGDOM OF HEAVEN IS WITHIN YOU

In the middle ages, there were many paintings on Church walls, of what was known as Doomsday, or Judgment Day. These consisted of human souls, the saints, beautifully clothed, with haloes of light around their heads, standing in orderly rows, in a garden before God. Below this, the souls of the damned were pushed naked and screaming into fiery pits, by demons armed with pitchforks. There was both carrot and stick here. Be good and the garden of God is yours, but behave yourself or else....

These were images produced by great artists, but artists who had split, primitive, childish minds, typical of their times, rather than an aid to adult growth of spirit.

In the sixteenth century, during the Renaissance, Michelangelo, at the request of the Pope, painted the entire wall of the Sistine chapel in the Vatican. This is the place where Popes are still elected, and it has Michelangelo's picture of the Last Judgment all over one wall. It is incredibly beautiful art, the work of genius, which we still admire, and visitors flock there by thousands.

Artistically, it was a huge advance on the comparatively crude wall paintings of two or three hundred years earlier but it had the same message - the virtuous in Heaven, the damned falling into Hell. Now, this is seeing the souls from the *outside*, seeing them as things, objects, about which you can make statements and call them "good" or "bad", saved or damned, sinful or virtuous.

There is, however, a totally different way of looking at the human soul. The only things we can possibly know about the soul with certainty are based on what we know about ourselves from *the inside*, because of our feelings, our thoughts, our dreams and desires. It is a fact that our feelings, good or bad, are always more powerful than our ideas.

People behave in all sorts of strange ways, many of them good, but many decidedly nasty, and the Church describes these as "sinful", but what Freud did, was ask the very simple question:

"Why do people do these things?"

His answer has turned the world upside down. Freud found that the reasons for our behaviour are not because we are born virtuous or evil; the reasons lie in our early life and childhood.

Now the Church also had asked the question "why?" two thousand years earlier, but with the limited knowledge of their time, came up with a totally different set of answers, which many religious people, of all sorts of religions, still feel bound to accept today. The Church has believed and taught that we behave badly because the soul is weak, we are tempted, maybe by the devil, or by the desires of the flesh, and because of "original sin" we are too feeble to do the right thing.

The reason for this was that the early Church was hugely influenced by Greek learning and clung to the ideas of the soul as taught by an extraordinarily influential ancient Greek called Plato, who lived about hundred years before Christ. Plato was a genius, a great thinker, with huge influence on the western world. Six hundred years later, St. Augustine, one of the greatest of the theologians of the early church, had an enormous respect for the thinking of Plato, which was based on *ideals,* things as they "should" be.

To see his influence even today, we have only to think of C.S. Lewis's famous story for children *The Lion, the Witch and the Wardrobe.* At one point, exasperated beyond endurance, the twentieth century professor exclaims:

"It's all in Plato, all in Plato, bless my soul, what do they teach them in these schools?"

PLATO AND THE SOUL

Plato was a philosopher, a lover of wisdom. He was a lecturer and writer in ancient Athens, about three hundred years before the birth of Jesus. Plato believed in ideals: ideal chairs, ideal tables, ideal men and ideal rulers. He was a pagan, and he thought of the soul in a very intellectual way.

Plato believed that the soul was in three parts;

- The Higher Part, The intellect, the brain, which can understand "the good".
- The Will, The Enforcer, controlled by the intellect.
- The Passions, which are very dangerous, and must be controlled by the Will.

Through Plato and St. Augustine, who studied him later, the early Church absorbed a split or "duality" from the pagan thinkers. *It believed that our intellectual theories, ideas, beliefs, doctrines and dogmas are good, but our feelings, our desires and passions are bad.*

Millions of people still believe this, including many Churches. It is believed that the intellect finds out what is the right thing to do, the good thing to do, and decides to do it. The passions however, the wild part of us, do not want to do the right thing at all, they simply want to enjoy themselves and have a good time, probably with wine, women and song. The ancient Greek philosophers were afraid that if the passions ruled, there would be chaos and madness in people and in society.

Since Plato and another Greek philosopher, Aristotle, who came shortly after him, most educated people (including the Church and also atheists like Richard Dawkins) have believed with the Greeks that "man is a rational animal." The Church has always seen itself as a defender of reason and ordered thinking. So does Richard Dawkins.

The problem is, that although human beings have tremendous reasoning power, in fact our emotions are always more powerful than our reason. This is why we have love and hate, wars, conquests, rebellions, splinter groups, rivalries, divorces, generation gaps, crime and punishment and addiction.

The twentieth century taught us that when we are in the midst of war, our reason helps us to slaughter more and more people with greater efficiency.

Plato said, and the Church said after him, that there is the Will, what we call "will power", which keeps the passions under control. St. Augustine believed that this could only be done with the gift of God's grace. We then have a controlled good person, a virtuous person. People who aren't very good at this are described as "weak willed", or maybe "degenerate" or "losers", and they are regarded with contempt. And so, thousands of years later, we human beings constantly beat ourselves up for not being strong minded. According to Augustine, everyone could be good if they would only co-operate with God's grace.

Women were always believed to be very inferior intellectually, with strong feelings but little reason. Many Greeks, and Christian theologians after them, believed that women, being irrational, were therefore more inclined to evil than men. Probably plenty of atheists and members of other religions believe the same thing.

Philosophers, believing that women were inferior to men in every possible way, physically, intellectually, morally and psychologically, believed that they were also more weak-willed than men (remember the fickle, ever-changing moon) and because, in history, women were always less educated than men, it was easy to patronize them. This innate contempt for women, sometimes kindly, became an important part of the church's attitude for nearly two thousand years, and its effects are still very much with us. It is probably the real reason why the esteemed female theologian, Tina Beattie, is banned by someone in the Vatican from giving public lectures on church property.

The reasons given are that Tina Beattie throws doubt on the doctrine of original sin as laid down by St. Augustine. In fact the whole Eastern Orthodox Church, The Greek Orthodox Church, and the Coptic Church (the latter in communion with Rome) all cast doubt on the Augustinian doctrine of original sin. Are representatives of these branches of Christianity to be forbidden ever to lecture on Church premises? It seems to me more likely that someone in the Vatican believes that the words "woman theologian" are a contradiction in terms, women are not theologians. Believing that women are inferior, enables men to think better of themselves. Of course this is not rational, but emotional.

There was an Italian Catholic cardinal who said that the reason why New Orleans was destroyed by hurricane Katrina was because of all the sin committed there (probably sexual and certainly all that disordered music). This sort of comment is the result of ignorant splitting. "They are bad, but I am good," and shows insecurity in the speaker. It is basically an unconscious feeling that bad things like hurricanes don't have to happen if only other people could have more will power, like me, and could control themselves.

The church taught for a long time that Man was made in the image of God, but there was an unspoken feeling that woman, because she was made from a rib taken from Adam's side, was made in the image of man (not very successfully). This has been the thinking – I should probably say *the feeling)* of the Church and mankind in general, for a very long time. Come to think of it, since the dawn of mankind, when Eve gave Adam the apple, or when *Homo sapiens* first walked out of the forest. The result of this is the belief that women must be controlled by men, in the same way that the passions must be controlled by will power.

PLATO'S IDEAS ABOUT SOCIETY

With his belief in Intellect, Will and the Passions, Plato thought that there was a similar ideal model for the organisation of society, and it was very authoritarian.

- The Intelligent Wise Ruler, a "philosopher king", who understands what is good, and what is necessary to be done. (Intellect)
- The Army (or Police) who enforce what the ruler decides, (Will power)
- The Ordinary People, called the "hoi poloi", the crowd, the plebs, the mob, the rest of us, the people who know nothing and have to be told what to do and made to do it - these are the human equivalent of The Passions.

Many a dictator or political party has believed this, though it is less intellectual, and more emotional than they might think. The central theme is the idea that the man at the top knows what is best for everybody. This is an emotional feeling, rather than a rational idea. The Church itself has followed this model of the "ideal" society for a very long time and it is the basis of the way in which the Church is still organised.

The Church has been ruled like a kingdom for centuries with the ideal, often unfulfilled, of a good, wise, authoritarian ruler, with wise counsellors and priests (acting as the Will) to keep lay people in line.

Plato believed that having a single wise ruler was the ideal form of government and I am sure that Hitler and Stalin would have agreed with him. However, the Second Vatican Council called for the Church to be more open and democratic. "Collegial" was the word used, meaning that all the bishops of the Church should have more input for decisions. Possibly even that bishops should be chosen by local churches, rather than the Vatican. None of this has so far happened, because the *emotions* of those in a position to organise things, are against it. Feelings are more powerful than ideas.

Because it has accepted Plato's ideal, (which fits neatly with human feelings of ambition) the Church has become a highly organised, top-down human institution, with the Vatican, or *magisterium,* at the top. The Church has lost Jesus' idea of a Church, like a tree of love and compassion, with huge branches and thousands of different birds nesting there. Instead, many think that the Church should be more like an army, with everyone obeying the pope-general's orders. This was the ideal of St. Ignatius of Loyola, the founder of the Jesuits.

I have heard (or read) it suggested that the Church is seen as a pyramid, with the Vatican at the top and the rest of us below. However, what has happened is that the top of the pyramid is still in place, but most of the lower two thirds has quietly moved elsewhere, leaving the Magisterium hanging in space.

WILL POWER AND DESIRE

Anyone who thinks that "the Will" controls our actions has only to think of many broken New Year Resolutions, or the "decisions" we make to be kind to everyone, give up smoking, lose weight and take more exercise.

Human beings do accomplish extraordinary things, and we often say that this is because of will power. But there is another way of looking at this, which is that we accomplish great things *because of our desire.* We are driven, not by our intellectual understanding, but by our emotions and feelings.

Feelings are more powerful than ideas.

I read recently that a young man who was an Olympic champion has been paralysed by an accident. He is determined to walk again, but meanwhile has already entered his name for the next Paralympics. He will undoubtedly need huge willpower, but the real driving force is his deep down *heartfelt desire, his yearning,* to be a sports champion in spite of his injuries, and his belief that he can.

Freud said that the reason some men can more easily triumph over adversity and be great is that their mothers passionately loved them, and believed in them. In cases like this, love is far more important than willpower.

A man may toil and labour all the hours that God sends, but there can be a number of reasons for this. It may be that he desperately loves and wants to support his family, or make a fortune so that he may never be poor again. The Bible tells us that Jacob toiled for seven years in order to win himself a wife, Rachel who he loved dearly. When he found that he had been cheated and given her sister instead, he set to and worked for another seven years to get the woman he loved.

A woman may stay by the bed of a sick child day and night, because she loves it so much, and desperately wants it to live.

An Australian film, "The Rabbit Fence" describes the epic journey of three very small aboriginal children, two girls and a boy, who crossed an entire continent on foot, following the wire fence across Australia, which was built to keep out rabbits. They succeeded, because of their desperate desire to go back to their parents, from whom they had been cruelly snatched away by the Australian Government, and put into orphanages. I believe the girls, now old ladies, are still alive, and I saw one of them recently interviewed on television.

DESIRE

It is *desire* which makes men and women sail around the world single handed, become astronauts, train for years in order to win a gold medal in the Olympics, become members of parliament, captains of industry, raise families, become priests or nuns or go to the moon. The Intellect may tell us how to do these things, and Will Power certainly helps, but it *is love and desire* which creates in us a deep need and determination to succeed. Do we believe that Jesus acted through grim will power or was He motivated by Desire?

The intellect often thinks that it is in charge, and often believes that the Will is of vital importance, but in fact it is the *feelings, and memories of feelings*, buried in the unconscious mind, which stay with us always that are the most powerful aspects of the human mind, causing us to do things, which often we do not want to.

My rational mind might tell me that I should give up smoking, but my unconscious mind "knows" that I really do need that cigarette. Probably, the reason I began smoking was to "fit in" with everyone else. I know it is not good to be overweight, but my unconscious wounded feelings need comfort through eating, and need it *now*. Who wins? Freud's explanation for these things is to be found in his little book *The Psychopathology of Everyday Life,* published by Penguin.

Not only is the Will *not* very good at controlling our actions, but the Intellect *is* very good at giving fake reasons why we do things. We call this rationalising. We may say that we vote for a certain political party because it has the right policy about the economy. In fact the real reasons may very well be that we like the look of the candidate, our families and friends have always voted that way, and we cannot imagine doing anything different because people of our social level have always voted in this way and it feels right. However, in some cases we may change our minds, but not without difficulty.

FREUD AND THE SOUL

Freud's picture of the mind, or soul, is also in three parts, like Plato's, but it is a very different threesome. He thought of it like this:

1. The *ego*, the conscious mind, which he called "the I", the bit of me that knows that this is me, the part of me which thinks, reasons and consciously remembers, but also experiences feelings of all sorts.
2. The *unconscious*, sometimes called the "Id" or the "It" – this is the largest and hidden part of my mind, like the nine tenths of the iceberg. The unconscious consists of memories of *everything that has ever happened, and every feeling I have ever had*. These memories are not all in my conscious mind, and I do not seem to remember most of them but the feelings in my unconscious mind, such as fear or anger, can powerfully affect the way I behave. This is where the passions we disapprove of live. Because of this, I do things I do not want to, or don't do things that I do want to, without understanding why. Freud thought that dreams often told us what these feelings are.
3. The super-ego. We can think of this third part of the self as the "parental voice". This is the voice in our mind, which belongs to our parents and teachers. This is the voice of the adult when we were children, telling us to go to Mass on Sunday, say our prayers, brush our teeth, clean our shoes, don't tell lies, have a bath, always wash behind our ears and – in my generation - children should be

seen and not heard. Freud called this the *"above I"* translated into Latin by an English translator as the *super ego.*

The problem with the "parental voice" or the "super ego", the voice of those who were in charge, is that parents, guardians and schools differ, and some are a lot nastier than others. This is why the mind can contain voices, which tell us that we are hopeless at maths, never in the right place when we should be, and always get everything wrong.

Over-controlling parents have children always haunted by the thought that they might have done wrong, either that, or they are over controlling themselves. For children of harsh, cruel or neglectful parents, the voices in their heads are harsh and punishing. The voices may say that they are stupid, they are ugly, a waste of space, nobody wants them, and everyone hates them. As a result, children become mentally ill, and may pass on the cruelty to others.

Another problem is, that if something really bad has happened in childhood, like your mother dying, the baby mind will probably think that "Mummy went away because she didn't like me", and the primitive unconscious mind *will accept this as true*, especially if the care after this is not very good. The child then grows up feeling valueless, and may feel like this for the rest of life, may indeed feel that he or she is a wicked sinner.

The conscious mind may say "Yes I am good", but the *feelings* of badness, of guilt and shame buried deep in the soul, may stay there forever and cause deep unhappiness and strange behaviour, without us understanding why. This can even lead to suicide. The feelings are far more powerful than the thoughts.

What happened in the past, for instance, to a young boy who wanted to be trained as a priest? Very often he was sent away from home as a small boy and educated in an all-male religious institution, a seminary, riddled with taboos and strict rules.

He may have been told, and really believe with his conscious mind, that this is good for him, a privilege even, but buried very deep inside may be the *feeling* that he is being punished for some reason. When he grows up his unconscious may feel that he must be very bad, or that he has to punish others. Making other people feel worthless may then ease his pain.

This is one reason why life is so difficult. I may *believe* something *with the conscious m*ind, but my unconscious mind is saying something completely different. My true unconscious desire may be at odds with my reasoning power, and *in these cases, the unconscious mind always wins.*

The only way out is to make the unconscious mind become conscious, and understand what is happening. I now want to try and think about the Church's unconscious reasons for doing things and because the church is composed of human beings, these are more about feelings than reason.

Chapter Two

Free Will And The Unconscious

"I cannot understand my own behaviour, I fail to carry out the things I want to do, and I find myself doing the very things I hate."

St. Paul. Epistle to the Romans. Chapter 7.

The traditional religious way of looking at the human mind is to say that we always really know what to do, and that we have free will to choose good or evil. Many people who are not religious believe this too. Once we have used our brains, our intellect, to show us the correct way to behave, the right thing to do, we should use our Will Power and do it. If we don't that is a sin and an offence against God. Non-religious people might say that someone like this is a loser.

However, from looking at the quotation from St. Paul at the head of this page, we can see that things aren't always so simple, and we are often split. If we realise that we have an unconscious part of our minds, everything changes. No matter how good your intentions, if your own unconscious mind is against you, it all becomes much more difficult.

The mind is like an iceberg, one tenth above water and nine tenths below. The conscious mind is available, and we know what it is about, but we are driven by the powerhouse of feelings in our unconscious minds.

A recent TV detective story had a sensitive and angry detective desperately screaming at an evildoer, "Don't you know the difference between right and wrong?" The answer is of course, "no", from an emotional point of view they don't know, they simply can't understand. The conscious mind may do so in theory, but the unconscious damaged feelings of the adult wrongdoer may be like the feelings of a small angry child, aged about two.

THE UNCONSCIOUS MIND

The great revolution in Freud's investigations was the idea of the Unconscious Mind. Freud didn't really invent or discover the idea, other people had got there before him. However, Freud brought to the attention of the world the idea that men and women have a part of their mind, which they don't know about. We are not aware of it, and we don't know what it is thinking or feeling, though we can often guess from our instinctive actions.

Once you have understood this idea, you can find things out about it, but you can never reach your unconscious, until part of it becomes conscious. This idea makes the whole idea of sin and free will much more complicated than we previously believed.

Now the church has traditionally taught that the human mind consists of three parts; Memory, Understanding and Will. This is a very intellectual way of looking at the soul. If someone loses their memory, have they lost their soul? In fact, we have seen that this idea is not necessarily anything to do with religion, the Bible or the gospels, but is partly based on the teaching of the philosopher Plato. Many of the great theologians in the early church had been trained in Greek scholarship, and they introduced this way of thinking into the Church. As this is central to the ideas in this book, I will repeat it.

- There is the brain, the intellect with its reasoning power. Plato believed that if our intellect makes us lovers of wisdom, we will automatically know what is the right thing to do
- Next, there is the Will. According to this theory, the Will corresponds to grit, or determination, enabling us to keep to a chosen course of action. However, most people believe rather carelessly in Free Will, meaning that they think we can easily determine what to do, and that this is simply a matter of choice.
- Beneath all these, Plato and the Church has taught, are the passions, undisciplined and very dangerous, needing to be controlled at all times.

As I said before, the idea of a Brainy Intellect, strong Will Power and Unruly Passions sounds fine, unless you are one of those people who has made superhuman efforts to give up smoking, lose weight, drink less, or take more exercise, and failed. Are we then simply people without Will Power? Or we have we Will Power which isn't really powerful, but feeble in some way?

The traditional religious explanation for this is that since the sin of Adam, human beings have become *disordered.* This means that originally, Adam and Eve had strong Will Power, and could do anything they wanted to, but because Adam and Eve chose to be disobedient, *our* wills have become weak. This is Original Sin.

St. Augustine of Hipppo, a powerful Bishop and thinker in the early Church, who had huge influence, insisted that this basic guilt for Adam's sinfulness, "original sin", is handed on to children through the sexual intercourse of the parents (rather like DNA) so that all mankind is sinful.

Augustine taught that because Adam sinned, we are all guilty from our conception, and are therefore born sinful. Because of this, we needed Christ to deliver us from sin and hell.

Augustine had huge influence on the Western Church which was headed from Rome, but the Greek speaking Church of the Eastern Empire at Constantinople, which spread into Russia, never accepted this doctrine of "original sin". For them, the original sin was Adam's, and we suffer the results, but we do not share in the guilt, and children are thus born sinless. This is still the teaching of the Eastern Orthodox churches.

Freud's ideas about free will are radically different from the traditional Christian teaching. The trouble is that your *conscious* mind may be wanting to do something important which your super-ego demands, such as making a phone call, or getting to work early, but your *unconscious* mind, full of fears and anxieties or resentments from the past, may be dead against it, and working very powerfully to ensure that you do not do it. So you don't, because at the last minute your unconscious mind makes sure that you have misplaced your car keys or the phone, and can't find them.

It works in this way. Someone who has been traumatised in the past by a series of unhappy phone calls, may consciously think "that was a long time ago, time to forget it". Or, they may have "forgotten" the fact, but the ever watchful unconscious is busy sending the message – *don't have anything to do with phone calls, It's much too painful,* so it may be difficult for that person to use the phone because of unconscious overprotective feelings.

LACK OF WILLPOWER

The same explanation applies in a negative way; you may consciously struggle not to do something which you believe to be bad. However, your unconscious mind which is much more powerful, and is desperately trying to protect itself, may have strong reasons, such as loneliness, feelings of abandonment or anger, why you *should* do this thing which you may really believe is wrong, evil, bad, or just not the way that decent people behave.

For example, a woman who knows that she should not neglect her children, or that she should look after them and feed them, may be in such a state that her unconscious mind will simply not allow her to do such things. Why is this?

If the woman had been neglected or badly treated in some way in her own childhood, her unconscious mind has learned the powerful lesson that this is how children should be treated. Or she may be so far sunk in depression that she cannot even think of her children. Her behaviour also turns on something which Freud called "the return of the repressed".

Even though consciously the mother has picked up different ideas since then, unless she is helped in some way, her unconscious mind may prevent her from doing those caring actions she believes to be right. This causes a deep split in her personality, which causes her to behave in ways which are not for the good of the children and may cause her and them much suffering.

Maybe she spends the housekeeping on drink and cigarettes (or books and concerts). She may feel guilty about this, but in a very literal way, unless she gets help from another person, someone who is kind and understanding, she cannot help herself. Freud believed that the only way in which this can be overcome is if the unconscious becomes conscious through analysis, talking about the problem, trying to understand, rather than merely condemning the bad behaviour.

So someone who "knows" what is the right thing to do, and talks about it, anguishes about it, may in fact be unable to do it, because their powerful unconscious minds works against it. St. Paul clearly wrote about this in his letter to the Romans, Chapter seven.

"I cannot understand my own behaviour, I fail to carry out the things I want to do, and I find myself doing the very things I hate... In fact this seems to be the rule, that every single time I want to do good it is something evil that comes to hand... I dearly love God's law, but I can see that my body follows a different law that battles against the law, which my reason dictates.... What a wretched man I am. Who will rescue me from this body doomed to death?"

Poor Paul. He could clearly see that his reason and his behaviour were at loggerheads, but not knowing about the unconscious mind, he was bewildered as to why this should be. However, he decided that the simplest thing to do was to trust in God and this obviously worked for him, and he concludes:

"Thanks be to God through Jesus Christ our Lord."

THE SPLIT MIND

The human mind can be badly split or behave as if two contradictory ideas were true. The doctor says I must lose weight or have another heart attack; on the other hand I have an intense craving for food, which is probably made much worse by my anxiety about having a heart attack. My unconscious solves the problem by letting me think that I am not eating very much, or maybe not allowing me to notice that I am eating at all. Many an overweight man or woman is convinced that they hardly eat anything.

It was because of this splitting, that in the past "error", believing the wrong thing intellectually, was seen as worse than the terrible cruelty with which the "heretics" were punished. When people protested about this, they were told that "error has no rights". The doctrine, an abstract philo-sophical concept was idealised so that the actual human being punished was seen as another concept, a non-person called "error".

Because of this sort of dissociation, we can have mass murderers, such as the Nazi Reinhardt Heydrich, who loved listening to beautiful classical music, especially Mozart. Yet it was Heydrich who organised the crude practical details of plans to slaughter, under the most appalling conditions, every Jewish man, woman and child in Europe, and the entire world if he could. He came from a great musical family and was a virtuoso on the violin. What psychological death happened to him in childhood, and what terrible scorn was heaped on him to make him eager to destroy y others on such a vast scale?

In fact, many of the worst Nazis, powerful grown men, seem to have been so desperate to please Hitler, that they behaved like small boys clinging to an insane, remote and harsh father who must be pleased and placated by any means possible. This was a projection of their own child-hood experience.

They projected all their rage and anger onto the helpless and vulner-able - Jews, gypsies, the mentally defective, cripples and homosexuals, probably based on their own unhappy experience when they were help-less and vulnerable. This sort of thing is what we call "split personality". There is no doubt that such states of mind really do exist, and many expe-rienced psychotherapists and counsellors will have worked with people who are like this.

Now, traditionally, "sin" is something for which people can be blamed. We know it is wrong, and we can be sorry. We may be told to confess our sins, and may be forgiven and this certainly eases the anxiety. This explains the problem, which many people used to complain about, that Catholics were able to confess their sins, and then go and commit them again. I think that the Church was being very realistic here. We can't do the right thing by simply wanting to do so but people do need help and support from somebody.

This why groups like Alcoholics anonymous, or Weight Watchers really do help, because they, like the best confessors, give emotional support instead of condemnation.

Our minds are split. This is why New Year resolutions are often such a disaster. One part of our mind wants to do something, but the other part, the unconscious, does not, and the unconscious often wins out. If, because of a harsh childhood, we are very badly damaged, the unconscious *always* wins out. Health clubs make a fortune from the people who attend for a few weeks in January, and then enthusiastically stay away for the rest of the year.

This is not lack of Will Power; it is simply Will Power in the wrong place. Our hidden, unconscious determination *not* to change lifestyle, not to risk starvation, is stronger than our wish to change. Part of us wants to change, or thinks it does, but an even larger unconscious part of us, terrorised by fear and anxiety, wants to do nothing of the sort.

How then can we bring about change? Advertisers know very well that IT *IS NOT OUR INTELLECT, WHICH TELLS US WHAT TO DO, BUT OUR DESIRE.* It is well known that an alcoholic has to be brought really low and be in despair, so that emotionally he desperately wants to change his life, knowing that he will die if he doesn't. Then the emotional support of the Alcoholics Anonymous can kick in, and change begins to happen.

NOT AS FREE AS WE THINK

This why the idea that we have perfect free will, and can easily do the right thing if we wish, is simply not true. We can certainly make choices and decisions, but these choices are often motivated by unconscious desires, prejudices, or fears, unsatisfied needs, or grief. These are not rational but emotional.

For example, the hierarchy of the Catholic Church is officially against homosexuality in all its forms. But to modern eyes, the sight of grown men praying publicly in long, scarlet silk gowns, partly covered with thin white garments tastefully fringed with lace, does not speak to the modern world of sanctity, but something quite different, distinctly camp in fact, rather like the English House of Lords.

I have heard of people who like this sort of thing referred to as "the silk and lace brigade". I am quite sure this would anger and distress the wearers, but the reasons for their actions are of course totally unconscious. However, it is certainly true that some of those priests and bishops who rage the loudest against homosexuality, are probably at war with unconscious anxieties about their own sexuality.

The unconscious mind often gives messages directly contrary to the messages from our conscious mind or ego. Marshall McLuhan pointed this out many years ago in his book, *The Medium is the Message*. He explained that the way in which we present something is more meaningful than the words we use, because although our words are reasoned, the way we act is under the control of our feelings, and our behaviour may contradict what we say. As my mother used to say when I protested about something, "Don't do what I do; do what I say."

The prime example of this was the old cigarette advertisement showing healthy young men and women riding the range in wonderful scenery, smoking cigarettes. This appealed to the feelings, even though we know quite well that heavy smokers often end up with heart failure, or in cancer wards.

To smack a small child, while repeating the words "Jesus loves little children" would not be giving the right message. And yet the person doing the beating might consciously be quite convinced that they were right. The real message ceases to be about love, and becomes a message that power and violence are allowable and a good thing.

THE REAL MOTIVES

"This hurts me more than it hurts you," used to be the phrase often used when beating a child, implying that the person doing the beating was emotionally damaged by having to do it. In the past, this was even seen as a religious duty, "Spare the rod and spoil the child." It is a clear case of the adult apparently wanting to do the right thing and love, while his unconscious mind is quite clearly showing anger, envy of youth and maybe even hatred. By their fruits you shall know them.

We know that the unconscious mind exists in the way that Freud knew. He analysed his own behaviour, and strange reasons for some of his actions. (See *The Psychopathology of everyday life*) He listened very carefully, over and over again, to his patients, and his patients made it quite clear that many of the things they did, they did not want to do. Also they said that they could not do many of the things they wanted to do. We have already seen that St. Paul felt the same way. He came up with the answer that God loved him anyway, and to just carry on, which is practical.

Many years ago, I entered religious life, not particularly wanting to, but convinced that I must. I think now that this was based on my problems at home at the time. My unconscious mind sorted it, as you might say by telling me that this was God's Will. But in the long run this solution to my problems did not work. Twenty years later, I broke down and left.

In many ways I did not actually want to leave, and even after I had, I kept telling myself that I would go back. But I couldn't. Of course, becoming ill was probably another ploy by my unconscious to get me out of a situation it had got me into in the first place.

Remembering the Laurel and Hardy films of my youth, I often feel like saying to my unconscious mind, "This is another fine mess you've got me into, Stanley."

However, we are not entirely at the mercy of our unconscious mind as if it is a cruel fate - as we grow up we can learn about ourselves and others. The damaging experiences of childhood are often healed, through love, friendships and partnerships so that we can revisit the past and understand ourselves and in doing so develop more freedom to act.

The church's dependence on the logical philosophies of the Greeks, or of the medieval scholastics, like Aquinas, can no longer stand as a support for theology, for they no longer correspond with what most people believe or feel.

The Church's greatest role should be that of increasing love, compassion and understanding, spreading the behaviour Jesus taught in the beatitudes, rather than teaching grim determination to believe in certain teachings. Of course if a priest received very little love, compassion or understanding as a child, he will have difficulty passing it on to others.

Chapter Three

Jekyll And Hyde - Splitting

Everyone has heard of Jekyll and Hyde in Stevenson's famous story. Dr. Jekyll is all that the ideal doctor should be, good and kind. But, when he deliberately drinks a potion which will release his inner self, he turns into a monster of depravity. As "Mr. Hyde", he rampages through the city of London, spreading crime, fear and chaos wherever he goes. Dr. Jekyll was a split personality. "Splitting" is a separation of our feelings from our thoughts, often called "dissociation". Obviously, Stevenson thought that our inner worlds, our emotions, were full of wild danger and sadism.

Severe "splitting" is a serious mental and emotional problem but there are much milder forms of this state of mind, which we are all liable to suffer from occasionally. It exists in all human institutions and it also exists in the Church, and is often called "dualism".

One of the main splits is between the Church's mystical side of liturgy, poetry, art, music, symbolism, love, prayer and meditation, and it's legalistic, doctrinal side, based on philosophy, intellect, reason and logic.

Trying to idealise a situation, while ignoring reality is a result of splitting. Idealising the Church on earth shows a lack of realism, and is a form of splitting. That is why priests who were dangerous to children were protected - when someone sees the preservation of an idealised institution or doctrine as more important than relieving the real agonies and sufferings of people, this is splitting emotion from thought. It makes ideas and ideals more important than people.

P. M. Webb

SPLIT OFF THE BAD STUFF

Splitting in the individual often begins with some sort of early trauma so that the intellect is split off from the feelings. This causes the person to be withdrawn from reality, because ideas, using the intellect, do not cause him pain as his feelings may do. In institutions this means that the official line may be totally different from the practice, or that rules are considered more important than the work force. This leads to huge hypocrisy, not necessarily deliberate.

In the past, for instance, there has been, and still is, much blaming of women for anything to do with sexual matters. Often some celibate men seem to spend a great deal of time thinking about the sexual lives of other people. Other people can be blamed for their failings, while the celibates' "virginity" is seen as a virtue in itself. This is splitting.

Recently, I came across a story which is a striking example of splitting and projection. A little boy, John, had been carefully brought up by very loving but strict parents. His mother insisted on correct behaviour and good manners at all times. He was a credit to her.

On his first day at school, she was of course anxious, and when she collected him in the afternoon, asked him what it had been like, and had he been a good boy?

"Oh yes Mummy," he replied, "The teacher and the other children are really nice, and we did lots of exciting things." His mother sighed with relief, but her son continued. "There is a very naughty boy though, his name is Tommy, and he threw the paint on the floor."

For the rest of that week the daily reports continued. John went from strength to strength, and one day he was even made pencil monitor. Tommy however pursued his evil ways. He broke the pencils deliberately and scribbled on other children's books, he spat at someone and one dreadful day he swore at the teacher. John's mother began to wonder if she had made the right choice of school. At the end of the week, John's teacher asked for a meeting with his mother. The teacher looked tired and worried and John's mother felt sorry for her.

"It must be very hard work," she said, "especially working with difficult children like Tommy."

The teacher looked up "Tommy?" she said vaguely.

"John has told me all about him, and how he throws paint on the floor, broke the pencils and even swore at you."

"Ah," said the teacher and a strange expression crossed her face, then, "I'm very much afraid there is no Tommy," she said grimly, "the naughty boy is your son, John."

Probably because of the severity of his upbringing, the mind of the good little boy John became split, and he invented an alter ego who could do what he liked, another, naughtier, more natural self. While still at home, this other child "Tommy" was hidden as fantasy, but once away from his mother's eyes he began to act out his rage and anger. If he is not helped, this splitting maybe a part of him for ever and wreck not only his life, but the lives of others, including his mother.

Splitting is a universal problem. Catholics are right; Protestants are wrong. Straight people are good, gay people bad, all men are reasonable, all women over-emotional. This sort of talk is the result of mental and emotional splitting and projection of our own problems onto others. It used to be said that "Error has no rights". This is splitting intellect from emotion. "Error", an intellectual concept, that is believing the "wrong"

thing was seen by the church as worse than the cruelty with which heretics were punished.

People sometimes talk about "loving the sinner, but hating the sin."
However, any advice or action which causes intense suffering to another
human being is a delusion. "Loving sinners" is about compassion and
respect, not tormenting them in the hope of making them better people.

SPLITTING IS THE RESULT OF SUFFERING

"Splitting" begins in very early childhood when a child is still a baby.
Small babies know little between extreme happiness (full tummy, warm
and dry and Mum loves me) and misery (I'm wet, cold, hungry and alone,
SCREAM). Babies always experience life as extremes, but most of them
grow out of it. (Mum can't feed me now, but she will soon).

If a child is repeatedly ignored, neglected or ill-treated, the splitting
may never go away, and for the rest of life, everything is seen as extremes.
Behaviour will be totally erratic, people will talk sanely, and behave mad-
ly. Moreover, we are all inclined to split our thoughts and feelings under
stress. This is the origin of the English "stiff upper lip".

We have been taught that the intellect, systems and ideas, are more
important than emotions, in other words that splitting is good. Maybe
we are all split to a certain extent, but there are times when it becomes
disastrous. We are often told nowadays that there is a split between the
right brain, and the left brain.

The right brain is more laid back, more open to ideas, it is more involved with relationships and spatial problems; it is more emotional, imaginative mystical and artistic – it makes easier judgments. The left brain,
on the other hand, is deeply involved with language and systems, order
and planning - at worst it prefers systems to relationships and places

order above the idea of kindness, or understanding. People, it is believed are by and large more under the influence of one side than another. Again childhood suffering seems to encourage the over-development of reasoning. For a long time the church seems to have been ruled by Left Brainers

A child who has suffered a great deal, one who has been repeatedly abused, physically or sexually, or continuously neglected, often splits off the pain and "forgets" it. It concentrates on practicalities. When the child grows up, it is then able to endure, or inflict pain on others without feeling that it is doing anything wrong.

One frequent cause of this is sending very young children, usually boys, to a boarding school at a very early age. Small children need their parents, even if they keep moving around a great deal. Children deprived of family love and affection at an early age develop a hard crust, and a very vulnerable inside. They are cut off from their feelings of misery for the rest of their lives, and therefore from other people's feelings. This also applied to the boarding schools known as Junior Seminaries, where many of our older priests and bishops were educated. This explains something that always seems strange to me.

REASON AND SANITY

We occasionally hear or read that someone who has committed horrendous murders is nevertheless "sane" and able to face a trial in court. The reason for describing this sort of man or woman as "sane" is that we have always believed that madness is caused when the emotions overwhelm reason. Looked at this way, insanity means a loss of reason. If we can reason and appear sensible, the belief goes, we are sane.

So we have no difficulty in believing that someone who runs down the street screaming, while sticking feathers in their hair, is quite mad. If however they are able to keep themselves clean, converse quietly and logically, read a newspaper, understand a bus timetable and know who the Prime Minister is, we are convinced that they are "sane". They are rational, and we are convinced that this means sanity, but we are wrong.

It is precisely this separation of mind and feeling – being able to do hideous things, while seeming to be reasonable and rational, that is the real mental illness, the real madness. Psychopaths are well able to reason and organise, but their emotions are completely split off. They are insane.

This explains hypocrisy, especially over sexual matters. A gay priest may be so terrified of his own sexuality, knowing what the official line of the Church is (and what his father thought) that he will go to any lengths to hide it, even from himself.

A priest may tell a woman that God loves her, and in the same breath tell her to go back to a violent husband because of the "holy sacrament" of matrimony but he is splitting his beliefs and ideals, his reason, from his feelings. How can anything which comes from a loving God be based on violence and cruelty? I know women whose lives have been wrecked by this sort of thing.

The priest who abuses the altar boys is splitting off his idealised beliefs and thoughts about the priesthood from his feelings. He still believes the right things, he has the right intellectual attitude and he is still a "good Catholic" but he cannot control his desire. It is this sort of splitting of intellectual belief from feelings and behaviour, which enables a man to abuse children without feeling that he is losing his religious faith. He desperately needs to believe in his own goodness. The splitting is often involuntary and unconscious, the result of his own childhood trauma.

Severe splitting is one of the main symptoms of someone who is emotionally or mentally ill. It is a psychological term meaning that someone is "in two minds". This does not mean having two choices, but having two separate states of mind, which exist at the same time but never meet, causing huge inner mental conflict and turmoil. In this way a man can condemn sexual abuse because it is Church teaching, and yet give way to his feelings for the altar boys, splitting intellect from feeling. We can see splitting everywhere, in ourselves and in the Church and politics too.

Multimillionaires who are grinding the faces of the poor can really believe that they are acting virtuously. This is why in more primitive times, "good" men, could condemn others to be burned to death for believing the wrong things, and therefore being "evil". Hatred of the evil, often a hatred of the self, is split off from understanding and compassion. Such judgemental splitting takes place in any authoritarian regime.

For people badly damaged in childhood, this severe splitting can go on for the rest of life, and this affects them severely. Those who are split may find it difficult to concentrate, become absent minded, or distracted, and later on find it difficult to understand the pain of others. So a clergyman may preach the love of God, and at the same time threaten with the torment of hell, those he considers to be sinners.

JEKYLL AND HYDE IN REAL LIFE

In England a few years ago, we had a real doctor who was very badly split. Dr. Shipman was a good, kind, loving husband, and seemed a friendly, gentle, kind doctor. He was enormously popular with the elderly ladies who retired to live at the pretty seaside resort where he lived and worked.

However, after some years, there were a few queries, and then, years later, (he seemed *such* a nice man) someone finally realised that there was a very high number of unexpected deaths in his practice. Finally, on investigation, it turned out that he had murdered by injection well over a hundred elderly, but still very active women, who had come to his surgery with minor problems. Maybe up to two hundred – no one knows the exact numbers because many people these days are cremated. Since then, the law in England requires two doctors to sign a death certificate.

Someone whose mind is split to this extent may be so ill that when they exist as one character, they do not know what the other personality inside them is doing. What had happened to drive Shipman to this incredible behaviour? Some terrible childhood trauma, obviously, had left him with a split-off need to kill older women, possibly his mother or grandmother – maybe even convinced that he was bringing them peace.

Because it was split off, it was probably a part of his unconscious mind. Intellectually he was fine, he was still capable of writing out prescriptions, and his male patients did not seem to suffer. Although appearing completely sane, Shipman was mad as a hatter.

Why did no one notice what Shipman was doing? For the same reason as bishops did not want to believe that priests were abusing children. It is simply because no one wants to believe that a doctor could be capable of such a thing, any more than we want to believe that priests could deliberately sexually abuse children. The same thing applies to abusive parents. Adults really do not want to believe such horrendous things about other adults, so we ignore the signs. Our feelings overcome our reason.

THE RETURN OF THE REPRESSED

The trauma becomes obvious, when someone who is quiet, good, kind and self-effacing suddenly turns and commits some hideously violent act. Some years ago there was a case of a woman teacher, devoted to her pupils and her ailing mother. Her pupils loved her and she was popular with parents. Her mother however, was vicious and bad tempered, and constantly humiliated her daughter, who was afraid to stand up to her.

One evening while the teacher was bathing her elderly mother, she spoke about some friends and her mother began to taunt her viciously, saying that she had no friends. Finally driven beyond endurance, the daughter ran downstairs, seized a large knife and stabbed her mother to death in a frenzy.

Now, people will always say that this sort of thing, which happens from time to time, is "out of character". But in fact it is very much *in character*: so far in, so deeply buried beneath layers of fear, shame and humiliation that the sufferer herself doesn't know that it is there.

This woman was so terrified of her mother, that all her rage and anger and hatred over the years and the desire to kill her were deeply buried. All her life, she had been terrified of her mother's viciousness if she rebelled. However, feelings which are so deeply buried have a very nasty habit of coming back to haunt us. This is what Freud called "the return of the repressed". When these feelings are finally forced to the surface, terrible things can happen, as in this case.

We all have a good side, but we also have a bad side. Many of us have anger, buried deep, somewhere inside ourselves. Unconsciously we may experiences anger, a desire to do violence, a desire to hurt others. But we are good, and do not like to think of ourselves in this way, so we bury our feelings, but it would be better to recognise our anger.

Many men who were sent to junior seminaries in their childhood are deeply split about women, on the one hand idealising their mothers whom they rarely saw, and on the other hand bearing unconscious hatred and anger for the mother who sent them away and abandoned them.

The more we try to think how well we are doing, and forget the angry, hurt part of our selves, the more we may be deceived. Self-deception is a part of human nature often seen in politicians. The Church too, splits off its dark side, and until recently tried to see itself in terms of idealised goodness only, "Holy Mother Church", but with many recent revelations about abuse, this will no longer work.

Deep unconscious anger may build up in a man who earnestly wishes to be a priest, but feels that unwanted compulsory celibacy has been forced upon him. The more he forces himself to obey this stipulation, the deeper he drives his anger. His unconscious anger may be such that later, he feels compelled to impose compulsory celibacy on those who come after him.

Anger and rage that is hidden, is dangerous. Children who are treated badly but told how wicked it is to show anger because they must be good like Jesus, are in a double bind, the anger is repressed, but may one day burst out at moments of stress, maybe when they are adult.

One way in which anger is shown may be in constant procrastination; intellectually we want to do something, but the powerful unconscious part of us really does not want to co-operate with the grownups, even if that adult is myself, so we constantly delay and then feel constantly guilty.

The Church is composed of people who all want to be good and try to suppress their bad feelings, so some of that repressed anger and rage is bound to be expressed in the teachings and customs of the Church. Telling people that they are damned for all eternity was one way of doing this. We know we are kind to sinners, and we would not dream of hurting them, of course, but they will suffer...

There was a time, a few hundred years ago, when European Christians of all denominations, would cheerfully slaughter Christians who believed in a different way to themselves. Excommunicating so-called sinners from the Church, the People of God, became more acceptable. Mentally sending them to Hell can seem a good substitute for physical punishment.

There are split Christians who see Muslims as totally evil, and split Muslims who see Christians as totally evil. There are also split atheists, like Professor Dawkins who seems to see all believers as bad and all atheists as good. How he can believe in the innate goodness of atheists, when the atheistic governments of Russia, China and Eastern Europe, were so renowned for paranoia, cruelty and brutality, is beyond me. No one group can be totally free from emotional damage, or vicious behaviour, because the problem is not what we believe, but what we feel, and that is a result of our childhood.

Professor Dawkins, like the Church, claims to be protecting Reason. Like the Church he can sometimes seem insensitive. Because of this he recently went public (on Twitter I believe) saying that a woman who was pregnant, but had discovered that the child had Downs Syndrome should have an abortion and try again. His conscious motives may have been kindly, but he overlooked the loving and often intelligent nature of Downs Syndrome children. Like the Church, in rather different circumstances, he has cut off his feelings from his intellect. Many parents of Down's syndrome children were infuriated by this crass statement.

Governments can also be split, because of the unconscious rage of the rulers. In theory everything is supposed to be for the good of the people, but very often, because of boarding schools, this is all in the head, not the heart, and compassion is in short supply because of early abandonment by the parents. Jesus was definitely not split in this way, saying, "He who is not against you is for you."

Christians can believe that other Christians are evil, and there are Muslims who think other Muslims are evil. There are ultra-orthodox Jews who rage at other Jews. Some Atheists rage against all the religions. Women are idealised, but unconsciously hated. Rage and anger is a part of the human condition, even if we are convinced that we are civilised. Because we project our feelings of rage on other people whom we believe to be "bad", we give ourselves permission to ill-treat, punish or kill.

People in this unhappy frame of mind see the "good" as an idealized version of their own ideas, seen not only through rose tinted glasses, but in glorious Technicolor with lights and bells, and the contrasting "evil" of others in hideous darkness.

RELIGIOUS AND POLITICAL SPLITTING

The terrible "Troubles" in Ireland, when both the Protestants and Catholics were convinced that the other side was totally evil, is a case in point. As a result of this way of thinking, many people felt free to murder one another and anyone else who got in the way. During war this happens all the time, and hundreds of thousands suffer. All human beings have a tendency to split, and in wartime it is encouraged and sentimentalised, "Our boys" will do anything to the enemy, to save the good folks at home.

The Church used to talk a great deal about "invincible ignorance", meaning that if the person I am arguing with can't agree with the Church, this is obviously deliberate wickedness on their part. I won't do the damning of course, because I am good, but God is just and he will do the punishing... People who think like this seem to believe that God is worse than they are. All Christians are imperfect, like everyone else, but Jesus told us to love everyone. "This is my commandment, that you love one another as I have loved you."

The founder of the Church, Jesus, said that he came to rescue lost lambs, that God counted the hairs on everyone's head and that we were all of much more value than the sparrows. He said the Church would be like a great tree, which would receive all the birds of the air. He looked for lost sheep as a shepherd leaves the ninety-nine of his flock to find the one that was lost. He said that just as a woman will sweep and desperately search the house for a lost coin so too, he would go to any lengths to reach out to people of any description, even collaborators, women of easy virtue and men who did not keep the religious rules.

In other words, Jesus was not split in the way that he looked at people, he brought wholeness and healing. In contrast, some of the people who run the Church sometimes seem to find this generosity of soul very difficult. Often they do not seem to find it at all. This is because of the way in which their personalities have been damaged. In the past, the Vatican has made many attacks on "relativism" which seems to mean that we must refuse to see value in any other ways of looking at religion or human behaviour.

So much church doctrine is based on the writing of St. Augustine of Hippo, that it is worth noting that St. Augustine, Saint and scholar though he was, seems to have been very split. On the one hand he was lyrical about God's creation, and the beauty of sexual relations. On the other hand he believed that this had been the case before the fall of Adam, and would be again after the resurrection of the body... Meanwhile in this real world in which we live, he believed that it was sinful for a married Christian man to make love to his wife, and that if he did it for love, rather than the express intention to have a child, that was even worse. This is dissociation on a vast scale, between intellect and feeling.

WOMEN

When it comes to women in the Church, as in society, there is rather a lot of splitting. Men are judged reasonable but women emotional, so obviously inferior. Men are sensible, but women hysterical. This implies that hysteria is a biological problem, rather than an emotional and mental one. I was told only this week, that women make poor historians because they get emotionally involved, rather than use their reasoning power. The mistaken assumption here, the false premise, is that it is wrong to have emotional judgements about the past.

Quite apart from the fact that men can be just as noisily emotional as women, (think of any football match) the implication here is that reasoning power is always superior to feelings. Psychology reverses this, declaring that our feelings are more powerful and important than our ideas. It is possible to believe that you are being reasonable, when you are simply rationalising your own prejudices.

The development of a deep spiritual life of prayer and love is a real hope, and is often attained, but it can only be based on deep human values of love and respect. These values are just as likely to be found in married people as a celibate clergy. We cannot bypass the human part of ourselves, and concentrate on the spiritual. Even St. Thomas Aquinas said that he was not a soul, but a human being. We are not pure spirit. We are human, with all the joys, hopes, needs, desires and sorrow and messiness that involves. We cannot assume that a priest can achieve a high level of compassion, prayer and spirituality just because of his ordination.

Jesus wished to bring wholeness and joy, not fear, guilt or hatred. The Good News is that we are loved by God, and in our turn we must love our enemies, love one another, love others as we love ourselves and forgive our neighbour not seven times, but seventy-seven times seven.

Chapter Four

Sex And The Church

*Thus a good Christian finds in one and the same woman
... to love in her what is characteristic of a human being,
but to hate what belongs to her as a wife.*

St. Augustine

Freud believed that the cause of many of the things wrong with humanity, and the cause of many neuroses, was an unconscious repressed sexual instinct. However, many people who admire Freud would no longer automatically accept sexual repression as the basic cause of most emotional difficulties. Mental and emotional problems are now often associated with neglect, violence or some other sort of trauma in early childhood, which may of course be sexual, but not necessarily.

Harshness from carers, unresponsive parents, illness, hospitalisation, death of a mother or father, all these cause huge problems for the child and can hinder emotional development. Parents who have mental illness, are alcoholic or drug users, or simply abandon the child – any of these can cause appalling trauma for the growing child and the results persist into adulthood, and pass on into the next generation, not through DNA or original sin, but the childhood environment. This includes men such as priests who father children and then leave them fatherless. From the point of view of the child's development, this is much worse than fathering them in the first place.

What is a child to think of a priest who abandoned him for the sake of his "religion"? What is he to think of that religion? Especially if he is told that it is a religion of love?

Perversity, difficulties and anxieties about sex, including denial, are also symptoms of severe childhood distress, and can be an indication of child abuse. As the Bible says "The parents have eaten sour grapes, and the children's teeth are set on edge."

Many people mistakenly think Freud believed that everyone should rush out and find a sexual partner. Nothing could be further from the truth. He was a respectable married man with a large family. He firmly believed that promiscuity, that is, constantly going from partner to partner for casual sex is a severe emotional problem and mental illness, a lack of maturity, needing treatment. He was convinced that the aim of psychoanalysis is to help people to have secure, well-grounded, long-term relationships. He said that he wanted people to be able to work and to love.

THE CHURCH AND SEXUALITY

Although the Church's teaching on sexuality seems solid as a rock, this is largely because of the mental and emotional splitting discussed in the last chapter. In many of its teachings, the Church has, over the centuries, often split human love and feeling from intellectual and philosophical reasoning about sex and marriage. This is a neurotic way of thinking and indicates vast areas of unresolved human anxiety. This was recently made clear in the laity's response to the Pope's questionnaire on marriage and family life. It is generally believed that the reason why the results have not been made public is because the hierarchy was too horrified.

The Church has two ways of trying to solve problems about sexuality, both of them about the Church's control of the laity, and neither of them really successful. One method is to split off reality and tell people to be "pure" and to eliminate sex from the mind and body. The other is for students of Church law, known as Canon Lawyers, to examine the theory, theology and philosophy of sex from abstract principles and explain to everyone what they should do.   It reminds me of a cookery test I once had at school – the girl who remembered the recipe off by heart came first, even though her baking was a total disaster.

Many of these theories come, not from the Jewish Old Testament, nor from Jesus but from the ancient pagan Greek philosopher Aristotle. Greeks like Plato and Aristotle were great men, geniuses, but their ideas about sex were often perverse by present day standards. Aristotle believed that women were totally inferior.   Plato believed in couplings ordained by higher authority, a sort or eugenics to form a super race. This was in great part because the ancient Athenian philosophers, as well as many others in the ancient world, held most women in great contempt and believed that friendships with men were superior to relationships with women.

In Ancient Athens, decent women were expected to keep out of sight, though Plato thought they should take part in sports, like the Spartans. Aristotle had a narrower view, providing logical, philosophical reasons explaining that women are inferior. Many men believe them to this day, but if we read the Old Testament, we find that the Jews had many heroines in the Bible, Sarah, Ruth, Rachel, Judith, and Esther. Ruth was so revered that she had a whole book of the Bible all to herself and her mother-in-law, Naomi.

Although we have a vague idea that everyone in the ancient world enjoyed constant orgies, this is mistaken and probably a result of our own projections based on Hollywood and the stories of the more dissolute Roman Emperors. Of course the double standard of sexual behaviour for men and women, flourished and many men had more than one wife. However, earlier, before the Romans, some important Greek philosophers actually believed that sex was a necessary evil, and that to enjoy it was the sign of an unbalanced mind.

This was splitting intellect and feelings on a grand scale and gave another rationale for despising women because they would lead men into evil. Often, Greek philosophers firmly believed that same sex friendships for men, sexual or not, were far more noble than marriage, because they were more intellectual.

THE CHURCH FATHERS

Many of the early Christian theologians, "the fathers of the Church" studied the Greek Stoic philosophy, which disapproved of pleasure. This is the origin of the idea, held for centuries that Christian sex could not be pleasurable without shame and was only for having children. This idea that there should be no pleasure in married sex has haunted Catholic teaching for two thousand years. The rules were made by celibate theologians. Unconscious envy perhaps.

One of the greatest Catholic scholars with a huge influence on the Church was St. Augustine of Hippo, (a North African city) who lived well over fifteen hundred years ago. He was a widely read man, a spiritual man and was also a great bishop and writer. He was also the sort of man who rushed to put pen to papyrus every time an idea crossed his mind. He had an enormous influence on Church teaching and spirituality, especially about sin, sex, marriage and celibacy. So important has he seemed, that recently, fifteen hundred years later, the Emeritus Pope Benedict has spent much time studying St. Augustine and has held annual conferences in Italy to study his writings.

As a writer, Augustine was the author of the first biography ever written, *The Confession.* He was a bishop in North Africa, what is now called Algeria, but was then an important part of the Roman Empire. Augustine was one of the men who really believed it was his undoubted duty to add a horror of sex onto the teachings of the Church. This is of course partly because of the time and circumstances in which he lived, and partly because of his own emotional pathology and sexual anxieties developed during childhood.

As a young man, Augustine had been member of a religious group called Manicheans. Manicheans believed that the soul was intellectual and rational and was good, but the body, which they identified with the passions, was evil. It is certain that although Augustine eventually rejected this group and rejected the doctrine, he was deeply influenced by it for the rest of his life, even after he became a Catholic priest and bishop. This can only have been because he felt drawn to it emotionally.

Fundamentally, Augustine always seems to have believed that the body was originally created by God to be good and innocent, but that because of the sin of disobedience committed by Adam, mankind, and sexuality had become horribly corrupt and sinful. He believed that because of sin, sex is now always "imperfect" under any conditions, even in marriage and could only be controlled by reason and will power. This shows the split in his mind between his intellectual ideal of sex and actual real emotional sexuality of ordinary people.

A married friend of mine, with a large family, said that it has often seemed to her that the Church's attitude to sex, is that it is all right as long as you don't enjoy it. This is certainly what the Church used to teach until fairly recently, partly as a result of Augustine's teaching.

The invention of the contraceptive pill has, for the first time in human history, given all women the power to control their own fertility, to decide whether they are going to have babies or not. This transference of power from men to women, who were once believed to be inferior to men in every possible way, is one reason, probably unconscious, why the male,

49

celibate Church has made a massive condemnation of the use of the pill. It doesn't seem to have much to do with the Gospels at all.

The distaste for sex, combined with the conviction that sex should only be used for conception, is the reason for the Church's total ban on all forms of birth control. Except that is, for the "rhythm method" which is so notoriously inefficient that it is commonly known as "Vatican Roulette". Many women find the technique of the rhythm method complex, demeaning and humiliating, and it has the extra benefit that if it fails, women can be blamed for not following the method properly. This may of course be the unconscious reason why misogynist theologians urge its necessity. (On the law of averages, there must be *some* misogynist theologians).

COVERING UP ABUSE

It is this fear and distaste for sex, which probably caused so many bishops to cover up the horrors of clerical abuse of children. It was not that bishops condoned what had happened, but they were panicking. To begin with, none of them had any idea of the lifelong damage which could be done to children.

Having been taught from their earliest youth that sex for priests was out of the question, and should not even be thought about, they were in a double bind, unable to think straight or try and figure out what to do. Strictly trained from boyhood not to think about sex, avoiding the problem seemed the only possible solution. If this became impossible, the only thing left was to hide it.

In the psychological world this is called "denial" and is often the sign of a disturbed personality. Because of our childhood, we are all disturbed to some extent and we all have our areas of denial which are often unconscious. For example, there is huge pressure in all societies to keep sexual abuse hidden and secret and it has been like this for thousands of years.

If there was sex with children, this was seen as lack of control in the adult, but not necessarily bad for the children, for it was wrongly believed that they would forget it.

This plays into the hands of the abusers who feel compelled to commit evil actions, and who, because of their own childhood difficulties, cannot understand or empathise with the suffering, which such acts cause to their victims. Neither can they understand the terrible destructive effects on their victims' characters as they grow up, because this would force them to look at their own problems and perversity, and that is too painful.

It is an obvious truth that over the centuries, the Church has carried out war against sexuality because many early churchmen believed that sex should be totally controlled by reason and will power (and therefore by men because women are not very rational). Of course false reasoning can be used to explain anything.

Along with this repression, was a split off denial and huge unwillingness for hundreds of years to discuss, for example, the existence of thousands of young prostitutes in London and other great cities of the world All of these must have had some customers, possibly even clergymen. Talk of "fallen women" has always totally disguised the role that men have played in the sexual exploitation of women and children throughout the ages. Men who use prostitutes are not referred to as "fallen men" as if it is an endemic disease.

THE INFLUENCE OF ST. AUGUSTINE

St. Augustine, the theologian and idealist, had a blind conviction that the only possible reason for having sex is to produce children. He totally ignored emotions such as attraction or repulsion. He probably thought it was better if there was no sexual attraction, or even if there was repulsion, because then there would only be venial sin. He taught that sexual relations with women after the menopause were sinful because there could be no children.

Children were the only reason St. Augustine could see for marriage. If there was joy in shared sexual love, he thought it was a cause for shame. He believed that he had been sinning for about sixteen years, because he had a partner, a concubine who was eventually sent away – possibly by his mother, Monica, who wanted him to marry a Christian girl. The future wife she chose was a girl barely twelve years of age who had not yet reached puberty – this was almost certainly because she herself as a very young girl, had been also been married to a mature man. This is a clear case of the "return of the repressed". After a two year relationship with another woman, Augustine eventually rejected this plan.

From his writings it is obvious that Augustine loved his first partner and needed her, but he came to see this as a terrible failing. Given the social conditions of his day, marriage to a concubine would have seemed impossible. His Manichean ideas taught him that sexual relationships were bad anyway, and he was haunted by guilt all the time. He did how-ever, have one son.

Augustine was far from being the only Church Father who had seri-ously weird ideas about women and sex. For many centuries, loving your wife "too much" (having too much sex) was considered sinful by many theologians – this was the sin of "uxoriousness". This was not the teach-ing of Jesus, but a seriously perverted way of looking at human sexuality.

Augustine believed, with Plato, that things should be "ideal" - ideal men (celibate), ideal women (subservient and preferably celibate), ideal priests (celibate), ideal marriages (sexless) and ideal sex (for no other reason except child birth and totally under rational control at all times). Admitting that this was impossible since the sin of Adam, he therefore saw all_human sex as "imperfect" and sinful.

"IDEAL" SEXUALITY

Because the Church has taught that "ideal" sex is simply for having children, and no other reason, there are powerful consequences. Contraception is out – either condoms or the pill. Gay sex is forbidden as seriously sinful and perverted, and not really to be discussed – certainly not in schools, thus giving Catholic gay children an enormous additional burden of guilt, not to mention Catholic gay adults. It is only fairly recently that being gay has been recognised as a normal human condition. Even now, according to conservative theology, gay sex is always considered perverse, which does not, of course, mean that there are no gay priests, theologians or even cardinals.

Plato's notion of Ideals, is in many ways opposed to ordinary good. The concept of "Ideal sex" (meaning abstinence) means that ordinary sexuality is seen as inferior. In many ways "the ideal" is always the enemy of "the good" because it is impossible to attain. Ideal apples are always better than real ones.

Passion, according to this antiquated theology, is regarded with horror; it is they think, a disturbance to the tranquillity of the soul, something to be subdued and controlled, evil, wicked, not nice. As a result, forbidding the use of condoms in Africa must have contributed to the spread of AIDS and HIV. Compassion for the sufferers, and those infected by them, is overruled by clinging to a harsh, sadistic doctrine based on philosophy, a typical split between reason and feelings.

However the Church, or magisterium, manages to split itself over this too, nowadays offering as an alternative, a wide-eyed naive idealisation of married sexuality, in the context of a very large family, regardless of family poverty or even living in squalor.

Idealisation is not real, it is an illusion based on failure to accept reality. For instance, we are often told that all mothers love their children dearly - but this is not always true. Most mothers and fathers do their best, with varying levels of success. Pope Francis himself recently said, in an interview given to the Italian newspaper, Corriere Della Sera, that if he was not mistaken, Freud had said that "every idealisation is also an attack." Meaning that the idealised person is not treated as an ordinary human being.

There are many emotionally damaged mothers and fathers who do not or cannot love their children. There are many who have very strange ways of showing their love, such as beating or treating children harshly to teach them virtue or forcing their children to fulfil the parents' own ambitions. Many parents do not seem to care very much and are indifferent. Marriages between men and women can be far from ideal, and can be a source of great suffering, even in "good Catholic" marriages. Gay partnerships can have the same problems of course.

THE HUMAN NEED FOR LOVE

Tiny babies are not born with sin, but with a desire, a yearning, a desperate need to love and be loved, to relate to their mothers. If they do not receive care and love from anyone at a very early age, they will never learn to love others, and at the worst, they will be seriously disturbed. Loving God is impossible, if you have never learned to love a human being first, usually the parents or carers.

This is why it is so terrible if a baby or small child is moved around from one carer to another without any stability. The child becomes unable to trust and love anyone in case that person is taken away – again. This is why junior boarding "Prep" schools are so damaging.

This need for others never goes away, it is a basic part of being human and a very important part of being Christian. If this yearning for love is not satisfied in childhood, its absence in the adult results in despair and depression or enormous anger, which may lead to violence or crime.

Some may believe that this basic need for love can be sublimated into love of God, but we have been told that we must love our neighbours as ourselves. If we cannot love others it is because we cannot love ourselves, and this is a tragic result of unhappy childhood experience. If in the past, some confessors seemed harsh and totally unable to sympathise with their penitents, this can only be because no one had sympathised with them when they were vulnerable and desperately needed it.

For a priest to tell a woman, who is habitually beaten and ill-treated by her husband, that it is the will of God, and that it is her duty to stay with him, is obviously deeply sadistic. Yet I personally know women who have experienced this in the past. Such priests ignore the enormous psychological and physical harm done to the children of such violent marriages, but such priests are also themselves the victims of rigid early relationships or emotional damage in seminaries.

HOMOSEXUALITY

Consciously, the Church has completely rejected homosexuality. This again is denial, for there have certainly been, and still are, gay priests and even bishops and cardinals. In the past the priesthood was very often an escape route for gay men who were under pressure from their families to get married.

I well remember a relative of mine saying to a single man in the family, that he should be ashamed, and that if he wasn't going to get married he should be a priest and do something useful with his life. Senior clergy must have known that this sort of thing was happening, but as with all other sexual ideas, few were able to accept the reality and certainly not talk about it, because they had neither the understanding nor the vocabulary. .

On the other hand, one of the ways in which the Church used to legislate against possible homosexuality in seminaries and other religious institutions, was the insistence in training priests, monks or nuns that they must not indulge in "particular friendships", by which they actually meant love, though no one was explicit.

This meant that in order to avoid possible homosexuality (not specifically alluded to) men and women training to be priests or nuns were supposed to distance themselves from any feelings of love or affection towards any other person at all. This is a horrendous demand, and if complied with can cause huge suffering and emotional damage.

NEGATIVE OBSESSION

If a man comes into a room insisting that he is Napoleon, the Emperor of France, and his wife is Josephine, we assume he is mad. On the other hand if a stranger comes up to us, repeatedly insisting that he is not Napoleon, not an emperor, has never been to France, and wouldn't recognise Josephine if he saw her, we would be fully justified in thinking him a little strange. In fact, he is probably just as crazy as the other.

In both of these examples the men are obsessed – one has a positive delusion and obsession, the other has a negative delusion and obsession, for although he keeps on denying his Napoleonic tendencies, he cannot leave the subject alone, and keeps on talking about it.

A number of people in the central management of the Church, the Curia, the Magisterium, have seemed to be similarly obsessed by sex – in a purely negative way. They try to ignore it, or idealise it, or thunder against it, or desperately try to control the sexuality of the world, but they can't leave it alone. This need to control others, to condemn other people, is a strong indication that they have deep personal anxieties with the topic.

The concerns attacked are sex before marriage, gay sex, sex using contraceptives, abortion, or allowing divorced to people remarry, (and should they be allowed to receive Holy Communion?) in fact they simply can't leave sex alone. They reject sexual education in schools, presumably in case it gives children ideas, for they would rather the children remained ignorant, because they themselves wish to remain ignorant. This is negative obsession. It is seeing Catholics as people to be sexually controlled at all levels, in case they break out. This is caused by the fear of the individual who unconsciously believes that if not kept under constant control, *he* might break out.

There is a theological argument against "in vitro" fertilisation that it is "inherently sinful" because the man has to masturbate in order to obtain the sperm. Now *there* is fear of being a naughty boy, and also a terrified denial of ordinary human sexuality.

The Church's rejection of adult gays adopting children, can only be based on ignorance of the fact that paedophiles are often heterosexual. To be homosexual, is different from being a paedophile. A Catholic heterosexual parent is just as capable as anyone else of abuse of all kinds, such as violence, constant contempt or sexual abuse. Vetting is the answer, not a blanket ban.

As a defence, the Church now urges that all children need a father and a mother. As well as being a bit late in the day, this is the ideal (again) but throughout history the ideal was far from the reality for many children. What about single parents? Are their children to be compulsorily adopted?

Again, Plato's "ideal" is the enemy of the ordinary good. By insisting on ideal circumstances, the church is attacking the reality of an ordinary, more or less successful family with its successes and failures, its ups and downs.

Children need to be taken out of orphanages, which are soul destroying, even the good ones. Historically, millions of children, including those in Catholic orphanages, have had to do without either parent because of wars, famine, plague and so forth. The important thing surely, is that all children need a "good enough" father or mother; they deserve to be looked after by someone who will care for them and love them enough, protect them from predators, but hopefully not exploit them.

Gender is not clear-cut; there are men who are more maternal than some women, and some women who have what we consider to be masculine traits. Freud believed that most humans have a tendency to bisexuality – witness the enthusiastic group hugs in a football match. Throughout history, thousands of women have had to be father and mother to their children, through no fault of their own. Who raised the children fathered by priests who "repented" and abandoned the child?

Thousands of young boys have been raised in Catholic orphanages and schools by celibate men. Presumably they needed a mother and father, but the Church did not see the need at the time. The Jesuits used to boast that if they had control of a boy up till seven years old, he would be theirs for life. These can only have been boarding schools for very small children. The Vatican did not disapprove and has never actually done so. No mothers there. The idea that a child needs a father and a mother, although worthy, has come rather late in the day. The argument smacks of desperation.

Many a child has been neglected, exploited, terrorised, brutalised, tormented, driven mad or sold into slavery, sometimes even killed, by undoubtedly legitimate, heterosexual parents. Many a woman has raised her children without a husband because the father is in the army or navy, working on oil rigs, "too busy" to have much to do with his family, or simply cleared off. Maybe the father was priest who backed off in horror, and retreated into his "celibacy". I have never seen a church law saying that men should not abandon their children.

CATCH 22

My first doubts about the Church's stand on sex, came at about the age of eleven or twelve, very shortly after the end of the Second World War. I was listening to the news on the radio and was startled to hear the newsreader say that there had been a new announcement by the Pope. The announcer said that Pope Pius XII had written a document exhorting widows not to remarry but to devote themselves to the raising of their children.

My parents listened with shrugs but this outrageous statement absolutely blew my eleven-year old mind. None of the priests I knew mentioned it afterwards in their sermons; so obviously, even they thought it a little odd. Feminism was still a twinkle in Germaine Greer's eye, most of us had never even heard of it, but my first thought was, what about men? Why had the Pope said women were supposed to stay single and not men?

Such was my innocence at the time that I absolutely believed that a marriage was fully consummated if Dad went out to work and Mum cooked the dinner. In fact my thoughts on the matter were completely economic – if a woman didn't marry again how was she supposed to have the money to raise the children? The early Christian custom of supporting widows seemed to have lapsed.

The fact that I had often heard priests insisting that a woman should not go out to work, but stay at home and look after the children, only made it all the more confusing. The sexual aspect of all this totally escaped me. I suppose the Pope came from an agricultural society, and had a vague idea that widows could all go back to the family farm.

I can't imagine that most adult Catholics took any notice of this, except to shrug their shoulders and mutter, "O my God, there they go again". That was well over sixty years ago, but it burned into my childish mind. Why women? It may be that the Pope thought that so many men had been killed in the war, that single women should have a chance to marry. Yet vast numbers of women and children had also died in "blanket bombing" raids or concentration camps.

I sometimes fantasise that because of an unwelcome marriage in the Pope's family, a relative had backed him up against the Vatican wall and told him to take a stand. Fantasies apart, however, from our present vantage point, it can only have been another unwarranted attempt to control women's sexuality.

One thing I am certain about is that to become the loving and generous, sympathetic adult he was, Jesus must have come from a deeply loving background. Not merely that his parents loved him and lived in the love of God, but that they loved one another. They must have done. It is basic knowledge for anyone who knows anything about psychology, that parents who are remote from one another cause problems for their children.

The gospels show no sign of opposition to sex. Nor was it a part of the belief of the ancient Jews, any more than it is of modern Jews. St. Peter, who is known as the most important disciple, chosen by Jesus, the first Pope, Head of the Church, was certainly a married man, for Jesus healed his mother-in-law. One of the few marital interventions that Jesus made was to protect and save from stoning a woman who had been "taken in adultery." His other recorded intervention was to produce extra free gallons of good quality wine for a wedding.

Jesus seems not to have been preoccupied with sexual matters at all. He did not stand on the steps of the Temple and shout about the evils of abortion, birth control or homosexuality. All of these certainly existed in those days, for among many ancient people, abandonment of the child was the simplest form of birth control. What Jesus preached was unlimited trust in God, prayer, love, peace, forgiveness, honesty, generosity, kindness, compassion, acceptance of the stranger as equals to the Jews who were his people.

Wanting to control the normal sexuality of other people is an ancient, cruel and very primitive way of exercising power. The earliest known form of control was castration, and in ancient times, thousands of male slaves or prisoners were routinely castrated. This occurred long before Christianity or even Judaism was invented.

It is worth noting that one of the early teachers in the Church, Origen, actually castrated himself at the age of eighteen so that he should not fall into sin. True, he was later declared heretical for his pains. Sexual control is connected to very primitive feelings of jealousy, envy, control, revenge, fear and anger, often unconscious. To make the negative control of sexuality such an important part of the teaching of the Church betrays huge negative obsessions and is straying far from what Jesus taught.

It is time for the Church to realise that the control of human sexuality cannot be, and should not be, the central aim of Church life. When Mother Church looks to psychology rather than philosophy, she may be delivered from such a cruel bondage.

Chapter Five

Compulsory Celibacy

*It does not profit a man to marry. For what is a woman,
but an enemy of friendship, an inescapable punishment,
a necessary evil, a natural temptation, a domestic danger, delectable mischief, a fault in nature, painted with
beautiful colours?*

St. John Chrysostom.

This is obviously the big question. There is no doubt that this is one of the central problems in the Church today. In what we like to call the developed world, there is a huge crisis of vocations to the priesthood.

For lack of priests, parishes are being merged and closed down at enormous rates. In my own Deanery of an English market town, we have had several parish closures and mergers. We are reliably informed that the number of priests will no longer be viable within ten, maybe seven years. Recently, two more priests have died, one of them young. We will shortly, in effect, be without clergy.

Whole parish communities have been destroyed and scattered to the wind, in the name of reorganisation. In Augsburg, Germany, it seems that four out of five parishes are being closed and merged. Lay people are being told not to organise Sunday services, but everyone is to try and attend Mass at central churches, miles from their homes.

The lay Catholics who have been running the parishes, are protesting vigorously but, as usual, they are being overruled by the bishops (who are probably overruled by Rome). Intellect and "reason" comes before feeling.

AN UNREASONABLE LAITY?

When parishioners in England are upset by the mergers, we receive a visit from the bishop's representative to remind us that we are very lucky by international standards. We are told that in certain parts of Africa, there are parishes where they have one priest to every few hundred thousand parishioners, scattered across parishes hundreds of miles long and wide, and most of the work has to be done by catechists.

This is of course, true. We had an elderly missionary a few years ago, and he told us a long story about how he had a parish covering four hundred square miles, in Africa. He was obliged, several times a year to travel by van or motorcycle, to every village where there were Catholics. This could take a month or more.

Once there, he would baptise babies, say Mass, hear confessions, administer communion and give children their first communion. He would confirm young people, marry people, and as the dead were already buried, he could say a Requiem Mass for their souls. The main point was that he couldn't possibly prepare people for all of this, so all of the preparation, teaching, advice, and follow up, not to mention prayers on most Sundays, was done by local African catechists, who practically ran the parishes.

He was obviously a hard-working man, but also an exhausted one. He had probably been sent back for a rest, but he said how desperate the missions were for further priests.

One thing stood out so obviously, that at first I was at a loss to understand it. If the African catechists were so capable and so dedicated, and if the Mass is so important for Catholics, why on earth couldn't the catechists be ordained? If they were, then all of this tearing around by van or motorbike would be unnecessary. It seemed blindingly obvious. More thinking however, produced a simple answer, the men were married - either that, or the catechists were women, and of course totally ineligible. Some people in power would rather see the Church die than make changes. Freud would call this an unconscious death wish.

NO EUCHARISTIC CELEBRATIONS

Back in England, when we complain, it is pointed out that we are unreasonable to expect Mass once a week, when we want it, and that in some places once a month is the norm.

It seems to me that you might just as well tell a sick man that he is lucky that the disease is not fatal; he will simply lose both legs, and maybe an arm. The truth is that the Eucharist, the one great central heart of Church life is being killed off because of the prejudices of the celibate men running it.

The one great advantage is, that many parishes in many parts of the world are now being run by lay people with a great deal of enthusiasm and efficiency, and to the spiritual benefit of all, but that will shortly come to an end in favour of gigantic "super parishes".

So what is the cause of all of this disintegration and collapse? The cause is completely obvious. There are not enough young and enthusiastic men entering the celibate priesthood in sufficiently large numbers to keep all the parishes going. Rome has in the past, set its face against married men as priests, and bishops cannot disobey this without being deposed. The Church as a centralised organisation has members, even bishops, who are not used to making important decisions, and moreover, and more importantly, they are not allowed to.

We are now encouraged to have parish committees. We have meetings at which parish matters are discussed and handled. In my own diocese and, I presume, across the whole of Britain, the creation of parish councils is being established. Some priests encourage this with enthusiasm, but others are rather ham fisted, and don't make a good job of it. This is partly because they were trained to believe that priests alone were essential to the running of the parish and partly because of their own emotional need for control.

Furthermore, at the one meeting which I attended, the priest began by saying that of course there were certain matters which were not up for discussion, because no decision could be made on this. This is a matter for the Church, and we know that certain suggestions would be totally unacceptable.

These suggestions have not only been unacceptable from the laity but also priests and bishops. Pope Francis has had to beg the representatives of the world synod of catholic bishops on the family, to speak what they think without fear. Religious leaders who have been obliged to follow the party whip all through their lives, are now having to be entreated to behave like free souls.

So what are these ideas, which cannot be discussed by the laity? Well, of course, we know what they are; we do not need to ask. These are about women priests and married clergy. We are back to sex again. Other forbidden subjects include birth control, but most young lay Catholics have already given up talking to the clergy about this, and make up their own minds. Many are leaving, or left long ago.

The point is that most Catholics see no reason why we should not have married priests, or even women priests. We want to go to Mass, and we want the sacraments. If there are not enough priests this becomes impossible. However, it seems that some people at the top of the Church pyramid would rather see ordinary Catholics without the Mass and Sacraments than allow clergy to marry. Again, it rather looks as if some powerful people have an unconscious desire to destroy the Church rather than lose control.

Never mind the fact that celibacy proves nothing about the holiness of the priests. The scandal of child abuse was carried out by men who were, in theory, celibate, so obviously celibacy proves nothing about holiness or even human decency. In fact some of the most loved clergy are known to have relationships with some woman or another. They become more human. The Vatican would probably rather that they did not become more human, but remain rigid in their opinions, and judgmental in their opinions, or even "live in sin", and go to confession.

A SEX MAD WORLD?

It would be very easy to say that the modern world is sex mad and apathetic to religion. It is so easy in fact, that many clergymen have frequently been heard to say it. In the unlikely event of priests thinking about Freud at all, they probably think of him as man who introduced the whole idea of modern sexuality and that the rot set in with his work.

Because of Freud, the theory goes, compulsory celibacy can no longer be valued by a totally unspiritual, unworthy and Godless generation.

In fact powerful men in the early Church, such as Augustine and Jerome, really did believe that the rot sets in with sexuality. They did not only think that celibacy was an ideal to be pursued by the virtuous man - it was deeper than that. What they believed with their whole hearts was that a virtuous man was somebody who did not have sex. If he had sex with anyone, including his wife, he was no longer virtuous, even if he was married and devoted his life to prayer and good works. By their weird understanding of sexuality, St. Augustine and St. Jerome were very unbalanced about celibacy.

This applies particularly to St. Jerome, a genius who translated the entire Bible from Greek into Latin, the version which was known as the "Vulgate" meaning the Common language. Jerome seems to have believed that women were evil from birth. But he was not alone, many of the early Fathers of the Church were contemptuous of women and sexuality though this was not biblical but pagan.

It is well known that Jerome had women friends, and these were mostly wealthy, learned women, who supported him in his studies by paying for his keep and setting up a home for him in the Holy Land. However, Jerome forbade these women to dress smartly or even respectably, told them to fast and pray continually, and to neglect their bodies. When one young woman died, some people blamed Jerome, for telling her not to eat. Probably he did not consciously want to harm her, but because of his childhood he was split.

It is fairly obvious that Jerome was terrified of ordinary women whom he could not control. He himself said that when he lived in the desert for a time, as a hermit, he was haunted constantly by sexual desires. He believed that he was tormented by demons, on purpose to destroy his chastity, which of course meant celibacy. Jerome, because of childhood experience, whatever that may have been, was obsessed by sex – in a purely negative way of course. His attitude had an enormous effect on the Church.

Priests were taught to see women as temptresses to be run away from. At a basic level, the supposed reason for this was that if a "celibate" man did have sex, it was obviously not his fault, but the woman's. However, most of these men were struggling, not only against all their biological needs, but also, and even more importantly, against the inborn childhood emotional desperation, for human closeness and comfort.

The less closeness and comfort a child experiences in its life, the more desperate is the frantic need for love in the adult when he grows up, and because of repression (which is unconscious) the more he will deny this need but the perfect man, according to the Catholic philosophy does not give way to this. To give way to a human desire for closeness is to be weak - but this is a perversion of reality.

There is at the heart of the Church authorities, a terror of sex and sexuality, which can only be called pathological. In their heart of hearts they are convinced that sex is impure, it defiles. This began in the ancient pagan world. The ideas of the later Greek Stoic philosophers in the ancient world were accepted as the mainstream wisdom by a church which became centred on Greek and Latin civilisation.

THE GOSPELS

Jesus, the apostles and St. Paul, as well as all of the important people in the early Church, were all Jews, though Paul wrote in Greek. Their early worship was all in synagogues. Before the Gospels were written, they used the Old Testament as their Holy Book. Jesus was constantly quoting the prophets, and we know that he read the scriptures aloud in the synagogue. But when Jesus was no longer physically there, a huge split occurred – a rejection of the body and concentration on the soul.

There is one way in which Jesus was different from all of the elderly hierarchy in the Church today. This is that as far as we know, he stayed with his mother and father all through his childhood and adolescence. He was certainly not shunted off to a seminary and raised by celibate men.

He did not stand in the temple or the market place shouting about the evils of abortion and birth control, though there were plenty of both in the ancient world.

For the Church, there is one major reason given why there is an insistence that priests must be celibate. Celibate men, it has been believed, are more spiritual and more likely to understand the message of Christ.

Frankly, the idea that those who are celibate are automatically more spiritual or holy, with their minds fixed on heavenly things, beggars belief. One of the main reasons why it arose is because of the assumed celibacy of Jesus but also the pagan Greek ideal of the perfect man. St. Paul, who had a very Greek education, also spread the idea that not marrying was a good thing, though he added the proviso that "it is better to marry than burn", not generous, but practical. Most priests have done a magnificent job of work, struggling with difficulties, but there are, of course, many who cannot really cope.

We know that St. Peter, the first Pope, was married because Jesus cured his mother-in-law when she was ill. However in the history of the Church this is carefully ignored and brushed under the carpet. We do not know if Peter stayed with his wife, or she with him, but, without a shred of evidence, the Church's implication is that this was one of Peter's early mistakes, and that no doubt he learned better later on. An early Christian commentator said that the "filthiness of his marriage" was saved by his martyrdom.

Some priests in history who were undoubtedly celibate, were unfortunately also undoubtedly power hungry, cruel and vicious. We can see that their celibacy did not even make them more human, never mind about more angelic. It is true of course that throughout human history extreme cruelty by everyone, including atheist governments, has often been the norm. The religious people were not necessarily worse than anyone else but celibacy did not make a cruel generation kind.

The result was that the Church believed that ideas and principles were more important than feelings. Being perfect (and celibate) was more important than grace, generosity, kindness, sympathy and imagination.

SEMINARIES

Until the late twentieth century, it was the practice to send young Catholic boys who wished to be priests, away from their parents at a very early age, and to herd them together in boarding schools, called Junior Seminaries, with a very rigid ethos

Having been deprived of human affection for most of their childhood, they were then expected to go out and preach a gospel of love, of grace, generosity, love of God, and the power of prayer. Naturally, what they often preached was a gospel of fear and caution, not sticking your head above the parapet, and total obedience. Some of them carried, a huge burden of unconscious anger around for the rest of their lives, which was projected onto others,

It is not celibacy which makes someone holy and spiritual, but the practice of universal love, generosity and respect for others. If someone has been raised by absent or uncaring parents, or uncaring teachers,, it is unlikely that they will learn to love, and they may cut themselves off from emotional attachment to all other human beings.

The Church's insistence on compulsory celibacy has led it to make bizarre, illogical and inconsistent conclusions. A Catholic priest who announces his intention to marry is dismissed from the priesthood. However, a married Anglican priest who converts to Catholicism, is allowed to go on working as a priest, even though he continues to live as a married man.

This last month, a priest who fell in love and wished to marry was dismissed from the priesthood, and left the people he had ministered to, and who loved him. He was replaced by a married ex Anglican priest with a wife and family. He is an excellent man and greatly loved, but this is still injustice. If this sort of insanity persists, the celibate catholic priests in England will be outnumbered by the very much married ex-Anglicans.

This is not only inconsistent, it is totally unjust, and to many Catholics, merely seems wilfully spiteful. A real Freudian might say it is caused by unconscious envy. Although good religious "reasons" are given for these actions, I fear that the underlying reason is that some of the elderly men in Rome who make these decisions have a rather sad and bitter unconscious mind which says, "We couldn't do such things, why should they?

There is one Church custom which clearly shows unconscious ambivalence about celibacy on the part of the Church. I once read somewhere that the bishop's mitre was developed from the tall headdress of the pagan high priest of Rome.

Whether this is true or not, it is clear to those of us who are sensitive to these issues, that, like the Old School Tie, it is an obvious phallic symbol. As such it represents male power and potency, which was adopted by bishops in the early church who were definitely meant to be celibate – compensation perhaps?

Quite how women bishops in the Church of England will feel about this I do not know – a bit of a puzzle. However, when someone pointed out to Freud the phallic nature of his ubiquitous cigar, he rather tetchily replied that sometimes a cigar is just a cigar. So maybe sometimes, a mitre is just a mitre.

Chapter Six

Paranoia

Fear not little flock, for your heavenly father knows all your needs.

Luke: 12:52

There are dozens of admonitions in the New Testament telling people not to be afraid. It begins with the story of Jesus being born. Even before that, an angel appears to Mary and says "Do not be afraid, for the power of the most high shall cover you".

In those days people had good reason to be afraid, for they were governed by a harsh military power, which could take people into slavery, crucify them in public, and send in the soldiers to solve any problem. The Roman idea of public entertainment was to see slaves fight to the death in public, mock battles between slaves who fought for their lives, for they would certainly die if they did not, and human beings torn apart in public by wild beasts.

These were real fears and we need to be afraid if we are to survive, but we all know that there are many fears which are not at all real. One of the most dreadful forms of neurosis, which can afflict anyone, is paranoia. Paranoia means irrational fear of anything and everything. The paranoid sees enemies walking down the street, in the school, the office and the factory. What he or she sees on T.V. is also frightening and really the enemy. Maybe, the paranoid thinks, the news announcers are really spies watching me? A little scepticism is a good thing, but constant disbelief, constant terror, constant dread is a nightmare.

The gospels constantly tell us not to be afraid. Paranoia makes people aggressive.

CONSTANT DEFENSIVENESS

As we have seen, one reason for this was that in the past, most of the men who are now senior in the church were sent to junior seminaries as boys. For centuries also, men who became theologians were raised in all male institutions, often in monasteries. A recently published book *Wounded Leaders*, by Nick Duffel, who has made a study of the effects of such education, states in the preface that:

"The price paid for the ex-boarder's passport to elitism is a defensively organised personality that is durable, if brittle."

As a result of this defensiveness, some of the leaders of the Church have seemed to be afraid of an enormous number of things. This fear of new things, of so many "suspect" things would be, in an individual, the sign of a severe neurosis. It is also the sign that something is wrong with an organization.

It is sad that an institution which follows Christ, who was constantly telling people not to be afraid, and who was not himself afraid, should apparently fear so many things. This fear is often masked by a concern for the faithful who must be protected at all costs from The World, The Flesh and The Devil. The "little ones" must be saved from the terrors and temptations, which surround them. Some feel that very often the faithful seem far less afraid than the priests who are supposed to be protecting them.

The leaders of the Church in Rome are given the grand name of "the Magisterium". The fear which seems to obsess the magisterium, is often fear of the new. Also fear of what women might get up to if not kept under control.

For instance, there always seemed to be a belief that civilisation will crash if women would not conform. As a young girl I sat through countless sermons by priests saying that married women should not go out to work, but stay at home and look after the children. It must have been the idea of women having money of their own that was the problem, because no one had complained about them doing farm work or working as servants in previous centuries.

Then there was a whole series of sermons about the evils of women, especially young women, who went to Church without wearing a head covering of some sort. Jazz dancing was pretty bad. Then it was going to the cinema on Sunday, and so on and so on. This need to control women, was accompanied by an unrealistic idealisation of the female, usually seen in sermons on Our Lady. Idealisation always conceals an attack.

By the time television arrived, they had to give up, after all they couldn't forbid people to turn on the TV in their own homes. And always, always, there were sermons against the materialistic society, invariably preached to people who possessed very little,   but most it was all *fear of the new*, and power, of course.

FEAR OF THE NEW

There have always been human beings, and elements of the Church, all Churches, and political parties if it comes to that, who don't like anything very much, and are always against anything new that happens. This is not rational, but a part of their own emotional difficulties. Far from *not* being afraid, as the Gospel tells us, there has been far too much fear.

Examples of this are to be seen in the anger directed at condoms, the pill, in vitro fertilisation and so on, even tampons, God help us, in case they were used for birth control. For people who are not interested in sex at all, because it is "unspiritual", they seem to spend a lot of time thinking about it

I don't believe everything that Freud said about God, any more than I would believe everything he said about cooking, but he did have a serious point when he said that people's ideas of God were based on how they experienced their parents when they were little children. Telling a child that God is a Heavenly Father does not necessarily reassure someone whose earthly father was constantly angry, bullying or vicious in speech. I think that many priests and bishops must have had rather strict fathers, or indeed mothers.

There is a story told by Father Gerard Hughes S.J. that there are children in a happy family who are told that they have an Uncle George, and that Uncle George loves children very much, and will do anything he can to make them happy. On the other hand, if they annoy him, he will banish them to the cellar where they will be punished with torments for the rest of their lives……..

Replace "Uncle George" with "God" and it is possible to see that some Church teaching in the past has often presented a God who is nothing more than a terrifying tyrant.

People going to dance halls, I remember, were once considered in danger of sin. Many, many years ago, I read a jolly little story in a Catholic magazine about a young woman who had arranged to go out dancing with her friends. She is to meet them outside the Church and while waiting for the car to arrive she sees people going entering and realises that she hasn't been to confession. After struggling with her conscience she goes to confession, and abandons her friends, who go without her. The punch line was that there was a traffic accident and all her friends, (who had not been to confession) were killed. Thus perish all sinners.

Don't enjoy yourself, or God will punish you.

I do not remember many sermons on the evils of heavy drinking, the evils of beating up your wife and kids, or the evils of cooking the books or cutting corners with the finances. There was however, a general idea in those days that it was a good thing if children were frightened and sub-dued. King George the fifth of England, was reputed to have said,

"I was afraid of my father in my youth, and I shall make damn sure that my sons are afraid of me."

There were and are, many like him. I fear that there are still Churchmen who feel the same way about God. "The fear of the Lord is the beginning of wisdom" is a suitable quote from the Bible for this sort of thing, but of course it all depends on what you mean by "fear of the Lord". In any case, that is from the Old Testament, and we are supposed to be living by the New Testament.

We need to understand that the Bible is not a single book, but an omnibus, a collection of separate books written over two thousand years ago. The Jews referred to it in the plural as "the Scriptures", the Writings. It was written over a period of several hundred years, by many different people. Some were mythological, some historical, some poetic, some ro-mantic, some depressed, some cheerful, some gung-ho and others in-tensely remorseful. You can find a quotation from the Old Testament to support anything, including racism, and many have done so.

There has been until very recently, and in some places still is, a fear and anxiety about ecumenism, that movement which encourages people of all faiths and religions to come together and try to understand one another. Officially however, ecumenism has been seen with qualified approval. Under Emeritus Pope Benedict, "relativism", seeing that other versions of Christianity, or other religions had their good points, was seen with disapproval.

All of this is a bit reminiscent of the Christmas Truce in the First World War. It was Christmas Day and there was not much fighting going on. The German and English troops were lying deep in ditches – sorry, trenches - in the cold and mud, and heard one another singing carols. One or two of them called out, heard replies, and after a short time, someone, a German, I believe, actually climbed out of a trench with a bottle of brandy, offered the other side a drink and wished them a happy Christmas.

Well, one thing led to another, and shortly after, all along the lines of trenches, hundreds of miles long, the soldiers came out into the sunlight and began playing games of football with one another. Sanity broke out, a good time was being had by all, and the junior officers who were there did nothing about it - no doubt they enjoyed the break too.

However, someone reported these activities to the Higher Command, both German and English, and soon orders were issued on both sides that all the men were to be sent back to the trenches under threat of severe punishment. Which they did. Discipline and duty was restored and killing one another resumed.

I often think that the official reaction to ecumenism is very much like this. OK. We'll get together occasionally, and be very jolly, but after that it is back to the Battle Lines. Don't let the troops get too friendly or they might forget which side they are supposed to be fighting – sorry, praying on.

Liberation theology, which appeared like a ray of hope and light to the impoverished and oppressed people of Latin America, was disapproved of by the Magisterium of the Church. I am sure they gave very good reasons, which seemed logical and valid, but the point was that Liberation Theology gave a voice to the poor and suffering, and it was suppressed with the full approval of the Vatican. The result was that people in these areas have deserted the Catholic Church in droves for the upbeat Christianity of the Evangelical Churches from the United States, and who can blame them?

The highly popular monastic community of Taize in France, is a community which has Catholics and Lutherans as well as other Christian faiths represented. Because of its enormous power of music, prayer, liturgy and spiritual renewal, it has been a magnetic place of pilgrimage for thousands of Christians of all nationalities and denominations, and especially for young people.

Catholics all over the world love the words and melodies, often used in Catholic liturgy, which come from there. And yet, a recent Pope rebuked one of the Catholic members of the community on the grounds that the place was not sufficiently *Catholic* in its theology. This sort of thing is not logic, nor is it about Christ, it is about a need to control because of deep personal fear and anxiety.

It is a terrible thing that an institution which prides itself on its devotion to the liberation of the human soul, should be so bound with the very human fears from which they are supposed to be setting everyone free. For paranoia is universal, we are all afraid of the unknown, the stranger. Those of us who had frightening childhoods, and we are many, are more afraid than others.

We all fear the stranger, because, as Freud well knew, *in spite of the veneer of civilization, we are frightened, primitive individuals, living in frightened tribes.* Given human history we have every reason to be so, but Christ's message of universal love – love your enemy - was supposed to help us bring an end to all of that. "Love", as Saint Paul remarked, "casts out fear".

As Freud realised, we are all capable of hatred, envy, terror, cruelty, and arrogance. If these things are blatant, because of the circumstances of early childhood, then the person is emotionally ill and needs help.

Maybe the elderly clergy of the magisterium did have frightening childhoods. For many, their childhood was after all spent in the hideous Europe of World War II and its aftermath. Or maybe they had strict or harsh parents or were separated from kind parents. At the very least, in those days they would have been sent away from home at a very early age to prepare for the priesthood in junior seminaries, which were rather strict boarding schools.

John Bowlby, an English follower of Freud, studied small children. After filming many examples, he came to the conclusion that the most terrifying thing that can happen to a small child, and affect his development for the rest of his life, is to be taken away from his mother even if he is kindly treated. The child feels abandoned, and this loss sets up fears and depression, which can last for life. There is then a desperate fear that the new carers may abandon us too.

Anyone who has seen the film The Sound of Music - practically everyone in the world by now - must remember the military way in which the hero, who had been a naval officer, runs his motherless family. He gives orders by whistles, and has roll call with the children standing to attention. I imagine that the reality was rather less charming than the film. But this was not seen as particularly abusive at the time.

All of this is caused by fear and harshness. Soldiers were cruel, because they were treated harshly by their officers. In the history of any country there are hideous cruelties, and these cruelties come about because children are not loved, and spend the rest of their lives taking it out on others. This insight is validated by the neuroscientist Sue Gerhardt, in her ground-breaking book *"Why Love Matters"*.

It is harshness and lack of love in our lives, which makes us as we are. Telling people that they are wicked sinners is not going to make them better, kinder, more virtuous or happier people. Sometimes it can make them feel even more guilty and more paranoid. It is kindness and generosity, which makes better people.

THE ONE, TRUE CHURCH

In my youth, one of the great Catholic organisations in England was the Catholic Evidence Guild. The Guild was founded by Frank Sheed who was an Australian publisher. The sole aim of the Guild was to train its members in the intellectual aspects of the faith, so that they could effectively argue in public against any speaker of any faith or none, and so convince them that the Catholic Church was the one true Church of Christ.

A favourite place was Speaker's Corner at Hyde Park in London, where crowds gathered, the hills above Bristol, the Bull-Ring in Birmingham or any similar spots in or near the great cities of England. The main aim of the Guild was to teach Catholics *how to argue* and above all how to demolish the opposition and show them how totally and utterly wrong they were. Not to pray, not to love, not to practice the Christian virtues, but to argue about intellectual theories. And argue they did, very successfully too. We were very proud of them....

In the sixth forms of Catholic Schools, the students were then taught Apologetics, which was simply a sophisticated form of argument against any theological position that was not obviously Catholic. It seems to me now that a Christian faith based solely on argument, is a very strange thing indeed, because rather than being open to others, it is based on fear of the opponent. The opposition must be crushed at all costs.

Can this possibly be the meaning of the Resurrection - arguing angrily with anyone who can't believe it as a physical event? if only we can stop being afraid - the doctrine of the resurrection is about the human spirit, rebirth, hope, creativity, trust in God, joy, faith in a manifest Resurrection of Love and Life in the universe. It is about our union with a risen god of love.

As a matter of survival we must love our neighbour – protestant, Jewish, Muslim, Iraqi, Iranian, Afghan, as we love ourselves. If we fear and hate them, they will certainly fear and hate us back. As someone once said, we must all hang together, or we will all hang separately.

Chapter Seven

The Natural Law

Aristotle is often said to be the father of the Natural Law.

Wikipedia

One of the most obvious ways in which the Church has separated thought and feeling, is in the doctrine of the "Natural Law". For Catholics, the "Natural Law" has been held up for centuries as the final court of appeal for all sexual morality.

Whenever there is a discussion about homosexuality, birth control, abortion or divorce, the hierarchy in the Catholic Church will always raise the idea of the "Natural Law". The recent Bishops' questionnaire, which has been circulating among the faithful at the wish of Pope Francis, (December 2013) takes it for granted that the "Natural Law" has an important part to play in the life of the Catholic family.

The idea of the "Natural Law" has a long and distinguished history. It was begun over two thousand years ago, long before Christ, by the Greek Pagan philosophers Plato and Aristotle. It was taken up a thousand years later by the learned St. Augustine, and eight hundred years after that by the mediaeval philosopher, Thomas Aquinas.

THE PHILOSOPHERS

Plato, ever the idealist, believed, and many others after him, that there is a universal law of good behaviour, shining in the hearts of all men and that all men seek after "the Good". The theologian, Aquinas, certainly believed that the hearts of all men (though possibly not women) inclined to the good, and that *by reason*, we can understand what the good is. As all of these men believed that women were not really rational, this understanding of "the Natural Law" was probably originally meant for men only, though no-one actually says so.

Thomas Aquinas, in the thirteenth century had an enormous trust in human reason, following the teaching of Aristotle. Aquinas believed that the true use of reason could never be contrary to revealed religion. Reason must be able to sort out all problems, including the knowledge of what is good under any circumstances.

So, by searching our minds for ideals (Plato and St. Augustine), and by consistent use of reason, (Aristotle and St. Thomas Aquinas) we could know what good behaviour is, the Natural Law.

It is even said that the idea of the "Natural Law" is embedded in that august document, the Constitution of the United States. Believing that government should be "of the people, by the people and for the people," the Founding Fathers of the USA were convinced that the rules for a good life were self-evident, and graven on the hearts of all men. In other words they believed in a "Natural Law" based on democracy and the rights of every individual to seek for happiness. However, this version of the "Natural Law" would have seemed very strange to Plato, Aristotle, Augustine and Aquinas, none of whom were democrats, even though two of them lived in Ancient Athens.

There is a dark side to this utopian vision, for it never seems to have occurred to the Founding Fathers that either black slaves or the Native Americans already living in the USA, should govern themselves or share in the freedom of the white men who came from Europe. The reason is that unfortunately, like many philosophical statements, supposedly based on reason, the "Natural Law" is always subject to the prejudices and assumptions of those formulating it.

Plato, Aristotle, Augustine and Aquinas were, although separated from one another by hundreds of years, great men, geniuses, great philosophers, and they have influenced thousands of people over the generations, and still do today. In spite of their brilliance and genius, however, they were all united by at least one fatal mistake.

Each one of them, whether Greek pagan philosopher or Christian Saint with the possible exception of Plato, was utterly convinced that women were inferior to men in every possible way – physically, sexually, intellectually, morally, spiritually, emotionally, psychologically and any other which way you cared to look at them.

This even extended to appearance - for the Greeks, the naked body of a man reflected the divine, for the Christians, man was made in the image of God, but woman was a failure, a distortion. Aquinas kindly thought that woman was a necessary distortion of the male, a part of God's plan, because after all someone had to have the babies and care for them but he believed that women are nevertheless imperfect, conceived when the wind was blowing from the south, a warmer and wetter climate, and therefore lacking male strength and reason. This was not actually their fault he thought, but a necessity of creation.

REASON AND LOGIC

These great philosophers and saints all believed in the importance of reason, and logic, but they were also subject to the common masculine prejudices of their age. In philosophy this is known as a "false premise".

Although the Church believes that deep down in each of us, (men, anyway) is a knowledge of "the good", and this is the "Natural Law", everyone knows that much of the Church's insistence on the importance of the "Natural Law" concentrates on certain types of sexual behaviour.

The theological argument insists that birth control, whether by pill or condom, or any other "artificial" means is wrong, because it is against the "Natural Law". Homosexuality is wrong, because it is against the "Natural Law". All abortion even for young girls who have been brutally raped, is wrong because it is against the "Natural Law".

Of course, for most modern civilised people, except by the crudest biological standards, it is also against the "Natural Law" for a grown man to rape a young girl or boy. However, following a classic philosophy in ages when girls were married off at very early age, rape was believed to be sinful, but not against the "Natural Law".

The "Natural Law" is an argument used by Catholic philosophers and theologians to say that certain acts are wrong, not because the Pope or a priest or even the Bible says so, but because it is "Against Nature". The concept is based on a highly idealised and intellectual view of nature, itself based on Plato's philosophy of Ideals and developed by St. Augustine.

This philosophical system says that we all know what is good (a doubtful point) but the Church has a split approach, first saying what the "Natural Law" is, as if it was automatic like the Law of Gravity, and second, saying that we should all conform to it, as if it was not automatic at all but a rule like the speed limit. Logically, it cannot be both.

Calling this a "Natural Law" seems to place the argument beyond religious discussion, and make it scientific, "It's not just the Church saying it. This is a fundamental Law of Nature and you can't mess about with Nature. This is science. This is how things are. This is how the world is. This is what always happens. This is the Law of Nature."

Only, it isn't, not quite.

THE LAW OF NATURE

The problem rests on that little word, "law". In English there are many words used for a number of different things. "Law" is one of them.

There are two main uses of the word "law", one of them meaning the observation of natural events, which never, ever change. This includes the speed of light and the law of gravity. This is the Law of Nature.

More often, in common speech "law" means a human rule, which, if broken, will result in punishment if the criminal can be caught but we all know that this sort of law is not at all fixed and unchanging. We talk of interpreting the law and getting round the law, or bending the law, and our cynicism is expressed in the saying "one law for the rich, and another for the poor."

For a scientist, a law is a description of some fact, which cannot be altered. The Law of Nature tells us what happens in reality in the world we live in. One of the most famous Laws of Nature is the law of gravity. Apples fall down, not up, and anyone trying to jump off a high building without a parachute, had better make their will first. These are the absolutes of existence. We can't stop it happening.

It is a Law of Nature that lions and tigers eat meat, and cows and sheep eat grass. Pandas eat bamboo, and refuse to eat anything else. These things are the Law of Nature and there is nothing we can do to change these patterns. Some animals are faithful to one mate for life; others are not. This too is a Law of Nature.

The "Natural Law" is not an unchangeable series of events, but is a concept, an abstract idea, a philosophical theory.

THE NATURAL LAW

Catholic philosophers and theologians have used the theory of the "Natural Law", in two distinct ways, which contradict one another. First, the law is supposed to describe what is natural, and happens anyway, and second to insist that we must all conform to it. The Church's version of the "Natural Law" is split. On the one hand it seeks to explain what always happens, as if it was the Law of Nature, and secondly that we must abide by it, as if it was a man-made law – again, it cannot be both. On the one hand, it seems to mean things that cannot possibly be changed, and on the other hand it means rules we must live by, but which are broken all the time. This is a contradiction in terms.

Because the words "Natural Law" are roughly the same as in "The law of nature" many people assume that it means roughly the same thing, and that things "against the "Natural Law" can't happen. But they do, all the time

By saying, for instance that birth control is against the "Natural Law", theologians seem to say that this is so contrary to human nature that it should not be attempted. Of course, birth control is not contrary to human nature at all, because it happens all the time and has been attempted for thousands of years, by a variety of means. The same thing is true of homosexuality.

In most societies, as in ours, some sexual actions, such as incest, are totally forbidden, and "taboo". Freud thought that the reason we impose such a strong taboo on incest, is precisely *because it happens so often* and we don't want it to. We disapprove of it so much, because of the effect it has on biological, emotional and intellectual development, that huge efforts are made to forbid it, and burn into people's minds that they shouldn't have sexual relations with close relatives. As a result, when the taboo is broken, people go to great lengths to hide it

Human beings have tried to limit the number of their children for thousands, of years, often because of the sheer impossibility of raising them all successfully. The most direct way in the ancient world was to kill the babies or expose them on hillsides or rubbish heaps, "entrusted to the gods", or more likely to hungry animals. Possibly they might just starve to death or die of cold during the night.

If the babies survived, they might be taken, farmed out, or enslaved. This was still happening in European cities in the eighteenth and early nineteenth century. It is still happening in many places.

In some ancient societies, children were killed as a religious act. We see this in the story of Abraham in the Bible and Abraham was probably copying the behaviour of the people around him. This is horrific by our standards, but certainly not against the Law of Nature, simply because it seems to have happened frequently. We know, for example, that the Incas slaughtered children and captives, so did the Nazis. Brutal and cruel though such actions were, nevertheless this is the way humans behave in some times and some circumstances.

To the astonishment of the world, no matter how many children are slaughtered in the USA, many citizens still strongly resist the abolition of readily available guns and ammunition. The real Law of Nature, as we all know, is red in tooth and claw.

The Law of Nature happens, and cannot be changed. Water finds its natural level, birds build nests and animals mate. Occasionally, under extreme stress, such as crowding, animal mothers destroy their offspring and this also is a law of nature. It is now well known that a new male lion in the pride destroys the cubs which are the offspring of the old head of the pride – not nice, but it happens and is a law of Nature.

NOT A LAW BUT A THEORY

The idea of the *"Natural Law"*, however, is an idealised, abstract, intellectual theory of what theologians and philosophers think *should always happen*, and therefore is used as a reason for telling us not to do these things. It is celibate men, whether saints or philosophers, who frequently have deep unconscious anxieties about sex, who decide what these actions are. Possibly, this could be along the unconscious lines of thinking that as they are not generating babies, in compensation they are going to make sure that everyone else does.

The "Natural Law" is not mentioned anywhere in the Bible, it is not one of the commandments, it is not in the gospels, Jesus never talked about the "Natural Law", and it is not carved in stone somewhere. It is a theory. It is an ancient philosophical theory, maybe a noble one, and an attempt to bring order into chaotic society, but nevertheless, it is a theory, not a fact.

Of course, there *are* things which we all think shouldn't happen, but it is an unfortunate fact that in modern times, the words "Natural Law" are only applied when the church is talking about sexual behaviour of which it disapproves. It has never, for instance, included child molestation.

Saying that birth control is "against the "Natural Law"" does not mean that it does not take place or cannot happen. It happens all the time. Saying that something is against the "Natural Law", is not the same as saying that it can't be done, or is against the Law of Nature. It is simply another way of saying, "I really don't think that people should behave in this way." It has nothing to do with Nature nor is it a law in any normal sense of the word.

The so-called "Natural Law" is really used by the church as a human law, in similar way to the speed limit. It means, "This is what we think you should do, because anything else doesn't seem right to us." This is a reasonable position, but it is wrong to use the word "law" as if certain actions are impossible or unthinkable.

Incidentally, I have never heard it suggested in a sermon, or anywhere else for that matter, that it is against the "Natural Law" for a man to beat his wife to a pulp, ill-treat his children, use them sexually or abandon his family. To my way of thinking, if anything is against the "Natural Law", it should be compulsory celibacy, but this does not seem to have occurred to anyone in the Vatican. It is obvious that theologians who use the idea of the "Natural Law", mostly use it in an arbitrary way when they try to control the sexual behaviour of others.

Instead of ideas and rules based on a so called Natural Law" we need a study of human relationships, respect for the individual, love and human behaviour. Intellectualising is a psychological way for celibate theologians to distance themselves from feelings connected with sexuality but it also seem to give some celibates a reason for thinking about sex all the time, in a purely negative way. Their feelings, are, as Freud would say, repressed. When under stress there is a time when these feelings sweep back, the man or woman may be overwhelmed. The trouble with repression is that it comes back to haunt us. As a rather colourful client of mine once said, "I pushed the idea out of my mind, and it came back and bit me on the bum".

This is another way of expressing what Freud called "the return of the repressed". If we push unruly ideas out of our minds, instead of trying to understand what is going on, the chances of the whole thing exploding like a volcano are increased. This does not necessarily mean that there will be an orgy of sex, but it may result in some form of breakdown, mental or emotional illness, what Freud called neurosis.

By treating something like sexuality as a series of ideas, logic or "Natural Laws" which must be observed, celibate Catholic theologians distance themselves from the emotional reality of sexuality and human behaviour and relationships. They seem to think of relationships as unruly passions, rather than a basic human craving and absolute need for love, approval and affection. They may even think of marriage as an ideal, so that Christian marriage becomes some wonderful, idealised, fantasy way of life. Pope Francis reminds us of Freud's words that behind every idealisation is a form of attack. Idealising marriage in this way prevents us from thinking of it as ordinary and human, and as a result, often rather messy.

There are people, gay or straight, who use sex brutally, savagely, and cruelly. This is because they themselves have been brutalised. As children, they have seen adults use sex brutally, savagely, cruelly, and probably been brutally used themselves. These actions are perverse, and they make for cruelty and unhappiness, and for this reason we have severe laws against rape and violence, though there are still vestiges of the idea that it is alright if a man is abusing his wife. By many people - often English judges as well as priests - rape is still seen as the woman's, or even the child's fault.

The idea of the "Natural Law" is the sort of idea that made it a crime in South Africa or parts of the U.S.A. for a white man or woman to marry a black husband or wife. The people who made this law, were probably convinced that all such marriages were "against Nature", but even then, sexual relationships between white men and black women were happening all the time, especially between slaves and their owners. It was the *marriage,* making mothers equal and children legitimate, which people did not want. The Nazis probably believed that it was some sort of natural law that Jews were inferior and should be exterminated.

If the idea of "Natural Law" were used consistently, one would have to forbid heart bypass operations, blood transfusions and intensive care units, none of which are particularly "natural".

REALITY TEST

If homosexuality were really "against nature", there would be no homo-sexuals, if birth control was really "against nature", it could not happen. Because our minds would be hard wired against it, we wouldn't even try. If abortion was really "against nature", it could not happen.

As it is, some Catholic Countries have made contraception and abortion illegal. What happens is that illegal and dangerous abortion thrives or women go elsewhere. So thousands of Irish women travel to England and Scotland every year for the abortions they cannot obtain at home.

Some theologians see divorce as against the "Natural Law". As a result of this, divorced Catholics are often denied communion. However, some women are used so cruelly by their mentally unbalanced husbands (and vice versa) that these marriages cannot in any sense be thought of as holy, or the will of God. To insist that women stay with bullying, cruel, violent husbands is sadistic. This sadism is the flip side of idealising marriage. To insist that someone who leaves a violent marriage and finds happiness with someone else is outside the Catholic Community, betrays unconscious envy and cruelty.

Anyone who thinks that orphanages full of children with HIV is a small price to pay for the principle of not using condoms, is totally defending himself against reality. Anyone who thinks it is acceptable for a man to infect his wife with HIV or some other sexual disease, in order to preserve the great principle of not using condoms, is allowing his repressed sadism to replace his idealised and therefore unreal beliefs.

To say that it is the "Will of God" is sheltering behind the worst excuse of all. It is saying that it is OK to destroy human beings, but not OK to destroy ideas, theories and philosophical systems, which seems to be the direct opposite of what Jesus taught. That is a huge distortion of reality. People who think like this are themselves often victims of a harsh upbringing, which makes them terrified to face real, painful facts and feelings for ideals are so much nicer.

For a valid Christian life, powerful human feelings and emotions cannot be brushed aside as "lower passions", to be kept under control, no matter what. They are the most important part of human life. There must be more to catholic theology and morality than sexual control.

It would be good if the Church could begin to think in terms of Developmental Psychology, instead of philosophy. Psychology does not blame, though it has a keen sense of what actions are harmful. It has respect for the individual, it looks to the heart, mind and soul, to bring love, help and comfort to poor broken humanity. This used to be the role of the confessional, but if the confessor was judgmental, it made matters worse. If the Church could study the hearts of men and women, rather than defensive philosophical systems of doubtful validity, it would be nearer to the vision of Jesus.

Chapter Eight

Sin And Psychological Evolution

Which is easier to say? "Your sins are forgiven you", or
"Rise take up your bed and walk".

Luke 5:23

I have suggested in the chapter on Free Will that much human behaviour which is alleged to be deliberately sinful, is often a matter of nurture, the way you have been raised, or often social or cultural circumstances.

Priests never speak about the Austrian Sigmund Freud, who invented Psychoanalysis at the beginning of the twentieth century. If most Catholics ever think of him, they probably think of someone who wrote a great deal about sex, which is one reason they believe, why the modern world seems obsessed by it.

The hierarchy of the Church and priests and clergymen generally, probably think that Freud is the opposite of all that they work for. They have a point; for *Freud rejected the idea that sin is deliberate.* I am not talking about nasty behaviour, evil, or crime, there is plenty of that around, but the idea of sin as a deliberate offence against God, for which one must do penance.

Many people would agree that it is Freud who is the basis of our modern, liberal, blame-free society. Why? Because he introduced and popularised the unthinkable thought that *people are not necessarily responsible for what they do.* And this is contrary to our philosophical notions of free will but as I have said elsewhere, our "free will" is very limited indeed.

Now, before everybody rushes in to say that this is against religion, morality, right thinking and the general good of society, I would like to remind them that Jesus himself very often spoke as if sin and illness were very closely related. "Which is it easier to say?" he asked. "Your sins are forgiven you, or rise, take up your bed and walk?"

There have been some clergymen, Christian and otherwise, who rush to blame the sinfulness of mankind for any terrible catastrophe. A Cardinal in Rome blamed the sinfulness of the people of New Orleans for the terrible flooding which destroyed that city. Many years ago I re- member another Cardinal blamed the inhabitants of central Italy for the dreadful earthquakes, which destroyed their homes and left thousands of them homeless.

There have been a number of American evangelical clergymen who leaped on the bandwagon at 9/11 when aeroplanes destroyed New York's Twin Towers - one of the claims was that it was God's punishment for homosexuality in the nation of America.

This seems rather odd for Christians. We are told in St. Luke's gospel that a tower collapsed in Israel with considerable loss of life. Jesus's dis- ciples asked him whether the collapse of a tower meant that the people killed were wicked sinners, or was it their parents? Jesus replied that nei- ther was the case simply that these things happen. God makes the nice cool rain to fall on the just but also on the unjust, and the too hot sun to shine on the unjust but also on the just.

However, some people cling to the idea that great catastrophes prove that sin must be punished spectacularly. Perhaps because it makes them feel less anxious. "These terrible things have happened to other people, but not to me, because I am good." This is clear in the Biblical story of the Tower of Babel. It was believed that because the people who built it were proud and arrogant, they were punished when it collapsed. This story comes from the very earliest written part of the Bible, when ideas were still very black and white.

Ideas about sin evolve and change, and this is important. Everything to do with human beings seems to evolve, to change, and in many ways to improve – sometimes things go backwards, maybe for hundreds of years, but somehow, eventually, we get back on track. We sometimes call this progress, and sometimes evolution.

EVOLUTION

Medicine has developed beyond the same bottle of jollop for practically every illness, to something very effective and precise, to the point where it seems almost like magic. Mathematics too has developed from the simple problem of counting the sheep and goats, to something almost mystical, that many of us don't even pretend to understand, though we know full well that it drives our computers.

Our ideas about religion and sin have also evolved. In the early twentieth century a French Catholic priest and scientist, Teilhard de Chardin, believed that the future of evolution on the planet would consist of increased, almost instant communication and knowledge, spread around the world. He thought and hoped that this would help to spread knowledge, love, peace and compassion, in the way that Jesus intended.

Teilhard died long before the explosion of smart phones, I pads, laptops, tablets, Skype, Twitter, Facebook and all the other digital paraphernalia that surrounds us, but the ideas he predicted are already happening.

However, like most human inventions there is a dark side, and these are often used for evil purposes as well as good.

These days, not many people who feel sorry or guilty think of offering an animal sacrifice in expiation for their failings, though they might send a bunch of flowers. So what about the evolution of the idea of sin? For most people this has changed enormously. The primitive idea of sin was that it was a bad act, which would offend the Gods, (whoever they might be) and who might be given to punishing us. Ancient Egyptians believed that their souls would be weighed after death. This idea is still very much around.

Later on in the development of the Old Testament, sin meant breaking a law. If you read the Old Testament, you realise that there were an enormous number of laws in the Jewish faith, easily broken. Even if you did not know the law, you were still guilty. We see this in Greek legends too. Oedipus was horribly punished for killing his father and marrying his mother, even though he did not know who they were at the time.

EVOLUTION IN THE BIBLE

The Bible was written over a period of hundreds of years, and even there, ideas modified and changed. Earlier books concentrated on not worshipping false Gods, not murdering people, offering sacrifices, and not committing adultery. Later books such as the prophets, emphasised God's mercy to all people and began to explore social justice, being honest, giving to the poor, and not being extortionate, caring for widows and orphans.

Gradually, it began to be understood that deliberately letting the beggar starve at your gate was as bad as killing him. Making a loan at extortionately high interest was just as bad as outright stealing.

Maybe governments and loan groups all over the world need to think about that one.

Jesus insisted that sin was often a matter of attitudes, rather than actions. He spoke of the harshness of the refusal to forgive and quibbles over details of the law, instead of compassion and kindness. He grieved over the closed minds of those who are constantly judging others. "Judge not, that you may not be judged."

Psychology shows us that such harshness and cruelty is itself a result of harsh upbringing and culture. In primitive societies, harshness is often the norm. Treating children with constant anger and contempt, teaches them anger and contempt for others, though the lesson may be stored in the unconscious mind.

One thing that has changed enormously over the centuries has been the attitude to cruelty. In the past, cruelty was often seen as necessary. It was thought that a harsh upbringing taught virtue, "spare the rod and spoil the child", but attitudes to cruelty have changed over the last two thousand years and most of us now think that harshness and violence towards young people and children is cruel and destructive.

CHARITY OR CHASTITY.

We can see this development clearly in the modern uproar about the Irish laundries. In the early twentieth century, young Irish women and girls who were pregnant but not married, were incarcerated in convents, sent to these places by their families, to work for years in the laundries, under harsh conditions, without pay, virtually slaves, in order to atone for their "sins".

Their children were taken away from them, against their mothers' will and through priests adopted elsewhere, often in the USA. At the time, the whole of Irish society colluded in this, in a desire to promote "purity and chastity" in young women, many of whom were sexually abused in their own families.

Today, most people are outraged, not by the women's "sins against chastity" but against the harshness, cruelty, injustice and unfeeling nature of the regime and the Church's role in all of this. There was no suggestion that any men were to blame. The children also suffered, and affected emotionally for the rest of their lives, being ripped away from their mothers' arms.

There has been a huge shift in the popular idea of sin but it is interesting that men still manage to avoid the blame, which has now settled on the nuns who ran the laundries. The fact that fathers, brothers, parish priests, senior clergy and politicians all colluded with the system tends to fall below the radar. For every baby there was a father, some of them no doubt the fathers, brothers and clergy and politicians in question.

We now understand that not only does cruelty inflict unbearable suffering on the innocent, but the cruel man or woman becomes brutalised. Treating children with cruelty and harshness can result in cruel children who become cruel adults, because they know no better.

Things have changed slowly over the centuries, and although stoning women did not disappear overnight, and in some parts of the world seems to be making a comeback, the idea that you can kill your enemies with the utmost cruelty is very gradually fading. The overwhelming slaughter of millions in the first and second world wars has changed our perspective forever. There has been an evolution of sensitivity, especially now that it can all be written about, filmed, and spread world-wide, watched on anyone's T.V. and computer.

In England over the last few hundred years, punishments have become less cruel and gruesome. Five hundred years ago, as in most countries of

Europe, burning people alive while tied to a stake was seen as harsh but necessary punishment for some crimes, including believing in the wrong religion. In England, up till the seventeenth century, people were still hanged, drawn and quartered in public. In England, the last woman to be burned alive for witchcraft was in the country town of Lichfield, in the eighteenth century but humanity is gradually turning against such terrible cruelty.

Because of our own psychological development, we are now more aware of the fact that much of what we consider to be sinful in human behaviour, is in fact caused by injustice, harsh upbringing and culture.

Last night, I saw a TV programme which showed a series of film clips of very small children falling over, falling off bicycles or swings or other playground equipment and in some cases falling heavily on their faces. They must have been badly hurt. The film was cut before the children began to cry, and the entire studio audience was roaring with laughter.

In nineteenth century England, beating children black and blue to teach them the difference between right and wrong, was not seen as evil, but a virtuous duty in many circumstances. Within living memory, savage beating of small boys was the norm but we have recently been horrified by a recent case in an immigrant community, where a child was tortured to death because he was suspected of witchcraft.

Nowadays, thanks largely to evolving understanding, we now think that there is something very wrong with the adults involved in such cases. Psychology tells us that they are horribly sadistic, because their own harsh upbringing has separated them from their own feelings, and the feelings of others, leaving them without sympathy.

One of the things that has happened throughout history, is the case of men trying to control their own sexuality by unconsciously projecting their desires onto women. It was not seen as a fault of men, or society, but the wickedness of women, that nineteenth century London had thousands of prostitutes, including very young girls and boys, desperately hoping to earn enough to eat.

Churches of all sorts were obsessed with the idea of sexual sins, or milder sins about "purity" and modesty. Because of Augustine's insistence on sexuality as the source of evil, the whole concept of sin was dreadfully skewed. For one thing, modesty and purity was something which was applied mostly to women. If a man had sexual thoughts this was often thought to be because some woman, or the devil was tempting him.

In the nineteenth century however, social evolution meant that people began to think that something could be done about these things. There were societies for prison reform, and orphanages, hospitals, and found-ling homes for new-born, abandoned babies, were founded. To every-one's horror, there were more abandoned babies on the rubbish heaps than rescue homes for them to go to. As in our own day, there are more unfortunates than shelters available.

In other words, people began to think about social conscience as well as the sinfulness of individuals. Individual Catholics and religious orders have done magnificent work here, and still do, with well-run hospitals, clinics and orphanages all over the world.

What had been seen as sin, which was thought to be purely the be-haviour of the evil person concerned, is now realised to be often a result of evil social conditions. The final invention of reliable birth-control meth-ods now means that poor people are no longer overwhelmed by enor-mous families, which they cannot feed or clothe.

ORIGINAL SIN

In Catholic theology, sins were divided into two basic sorts – original sin and actual sin. Original sin is the "stain or guilt" of sin which we have inherited from Adam. The aggressiveness, cruelty, brutality, greed for power and riches seemed to be bred in the bone. It is in the spiritual genes as it were.

You can see why the idea of original sin seemed to explain why human beings do such terrible things to one another but the word "sin" implies guilt, and the very notion of "original sin" makes us guilty before we are even born. One thousand five hundred years ago, St. Augustine taught exactly that, but Jesus had said nothing about it (and the Eastern Church still does not accept this doctrine.)

For Augustine, infant baptism was supposed to wash away the "stain" of original sin, because he was convinced that we were guilty of sin from the hour we were conceived. We now realise that this tells us far more about Augustine's own pathological sense of guilt, rather than the guilt of babies.

For many modern Catholics, the most important aspect of Baptism in modern days is that baptism makes the child a part of the Christian community, which is consciously striving against evil. Hopefully, the baby will be raised with love and compassion, and will therefore develop a compassionate conscience.

As we have seen in the chapter on the unconscious, very few of our actions are deliberate. Many of the things we do, or do not do, are stirred up by our unconscious desires and conflicts, and most of these things depend on what sort of upbringing we have had. Other things we do, that are imprinted on our minds, are the results of cultural training. Many of the things which are seen as evil now, such as the glorification of war, were not seen in that way one hundred years ago.

It is Freud who has helped us to understand our own deep motives and to understand the real reasons why terrible things happen.

ADULT BLINDNESS

When Freud began to talk about adults having sex with children, the idea seemed so monstrous to a respectable nineteenth century public, that no one wanted to believe him, even though the people he talked to were a mostly doctors. So, in despair at being misunderstood, and treated as a sex-mad offender himself, he gave up talking about it, and worked on other theories.

When the idea was revived in the last thirty or forty years, the response from the accused adults was mostly denial and hysteria. Court cases were brought by guilty men, fathers and close relatives, who blamed the counsellors and therapists for stirring up hysteria in young women, and "false memory syndrome".

Bishops were not the only men who refused to believe in sexual child abuse, and who protected their own. Governments and other organisations such as the BBC have had similar problems. The medical men to whom Freud first talked about these things, refused to listen to him either. Maybe the temptations for a medical man, and the need to be seen as above reproach, are the same as those for a priest.

There is no doubt that terribly wicked and evil things happen. Massacres on an unbelievable scale have taken place in the last few centuries – such as the slaughter of "red Indians" in America. Indians, Africans and Chinese were slaughtered and enslaved in the nineteenth century rush to create European empires. In the twentieth century, Millions of Jews, Poles, Gypsies, mentally sick people and homosexuals died in the unspeakable Nazi extermination camps. Millions more were killed at Stalin's decree in Siberia. There have been other examples since then. Every continent has its share of so called "ethnic cleansing",

Long ago, St. Thomas Aquinas reasoned that there is such a thing as a "Just War." He argued that if the situation is desperate, and one's intentions are just, humans are justified in fighting one another. This again helps to separate feelings and emotions from the intellect.

Aquinas may have been right in theory, but the trouble is that every single war-leader on earth, from Alexander the Great through Napoleon, Stalin and Hitler, thinks that he has just reasons for fighting others. Even the Nazis, perverted, twisted and vicious though their thinking was, believed that they were justified. It seems to me that the only thing that can prevent war is not a philosophical idea about a just war, but a passionate desire for peace.

Evil things happen because children have suffered, and they then pass it on in the next generation.

Chapter Nine

The Devil And Hell

The Devil, a supernatural entity that is the personification of evil and the enemy of God and mankind.

Wikipedia

Sure, the Devil's not such a bad fella when you get to know him.

Irish saying

This very week, as I write, a young boy who battered his mother to death was described, by one of the popular English daily papers, as "DEVIL CHILD," in screaming large headlines. This is obviously for dramatic effect, because I very much doubt if the editor believes in God or the Devil. The other reason is to help the readers feel good about themselves and arouse feelings of hatred (we would never do a thing like that, we are good).

According to traditional Catholic teaching, there are three enemies of the human soul – the World, The Flesh and the Devil. The first two make sense even to the unbeliever. The World seems to involve greed, selfishness and naked ambition. The Flesh involves exploitation of sensuality, pornography, promiscuity, gluttony, decadence and exploitation of others.

The third is a belief in a supernatural person, the Devil, Satan, the Enemy, Lucifer, Old Nick, The Prince of Darkness and Evil Prince of this world. At Catholic Baptisms, the child's parents and godparents are asked to reject "Satan, and all his works and pomps". In most congregations, the people join in, saying, "We do renounce him", though whether they all believe in an evil spirit called the Devil, is doubtful.

One ancient story is that Lucifer was a mighty Angel whose name means "Light", who once reigned in Heaven. In a burst of arrogant pride, he refused to serve God, saying, "I will not serve", and for this he was cast down to Hell.

We all have lurid visions of what Hell is like but according to the theologian St. Thomas Aquinas, Hell is not a place at all, but a spiritual state of eternal hatred, totally without love, and this is still official Catholic doctrine. Nevertheless, the popular idea of burning fires, and horned devils with pitchforks still persists and we are all aware of it. Many mediaeval paintings on Church walls and in illuminated books presented this image.

It must be said, that in Terry Pratchet's joyful book *Faust/Eric,* Hell is seen as a modern office full of targets and mission statements, devils who ask if they can help you and then tell you to have a nice day. John Paul Sartre, on the other hand, said that, "Hell is other people".

The atheist writer, Richard Dawkins, states quite baldly in *The Selfish Gene*, that the idea of the Devil was a story, thought up by catholic clergy determined to keep power over the peasants and frighten them into submission. He believes that modern priests still do so. However in many parts of the world, priests believe in the Devil themselves, so obviously they aren't or weren't inventing it. In fact many people who were not Catholics also believed in the Devil. Belief in demons came long before Christianity.

Two of the greatest English writers of the seventeenth century, John Bunyan and John Milton, both puritans and haters of the Catholic Church, neither of whom were clergy, both firmly believed in Satan. Milton said that his great poem, *Paradise Lost* was written to praise God, but most of the poem is about the fallen angel Lucifer, who is a powerful, mighty and even noble figure. William Blake, another great poet, said that Milton "was of the Devil's party, without realising it".

It is easy to make a film which will rake in the cash and break Box Office Records. Simply make a film about the Devil possessing people – usually a beautiful and sensuous woman, or an innocent looking little child, or several children if it comes to that. This of course reinforces a popular male prejudice that women are devils who will destroy you, and the general adult prejudice that young people in gangs are devils who need to have the evil spirit driven out of them.

PROJECTION

This projection of adult sexual prurience, anger and hatred onto children has been a constant factor in the history of man and womankind. One result has been to make harsh parenting and harsh education seem a virtue.

There is now in England, imported from the USA, a so-called "Christian" commune, who call themselves the "Twelve Tribes". Adults of the community ritually beat their children with willow rods, "to drive out the devil". They also deprive their children of higher education, saying that they believe in practical learning. Presumably, any child who shows a preference for college has the devil beaten out of her.

A journalist infiltrated a similar commune in Germany, and took pictures of six adults beating six children in a cellar, with a total of eighty-three strokes of the cane. He filmed fifty such beatings in total. Whatever the commune may say, such a regime is based on subconscious hatred and anger, not love. Because of the suffering of his own childhood, the founder of such a community must contain vast amounts of rage and hatred within him.

There have been several notorious cases recently in England. In some immigrant communities, children have been beaten and tortured to death, in order to "drive out the devil," which was supposed to possess the children, and turned them into witches. This is a classic case of adults suffering mental illness, and projecting their own damaged personalities onto the innocent child who has no defence,

The Catholic journalist, Peter Stanford made a noble effort to get to grips with the idea of Satan in his book *The Devil: a Biography.* This well-researched book traces beliefs and images of the Devil throughout the last several thousand years. Stanford does a good job, and touches on the psychological reason why we believe such things, also searching for the origins of human evil.

In his anger against the church, the atheist writer Dawkins fails to ask "why?" Why are people so easily scared? If I start telling stories about man-eating lions, no one will be fazed, so what is it about devils? Probably because we can see the lion, but the devil is invisible, and therefore can be anywhere without us knowing.

Dawkins assumes that a self-serving priesthood is determined to terrify the populace with the horrors of spending eternity burning in what Shakespeare called, "the everlasting bonfire". If this is true, why are they able to get away with it? What is it about human beings that makes them so easily terrified by something that they have never seen?

MACBETH

Four hundred years ago Shakespeare wrote a play about witches who worshipped Satan and led the hero Macbeth to commit murder, betrayal, and slaughter of the innocent. Shakespeare did this because the King, James I (once described as the "wisest fool in Christendom") had written a book about witches who worship the devil, and how to recognise them. King James, Head of the Church of England, believed himself to be an authority on the topic.

The play was enormously popular and still is. It is regularly studied for school examinations. No doubt King James approved of it, because it contains all the ideas in his book. There is, even now, an actors' superstition that because Lady Macbeth on stage passionately calls to the devil to possess her, Satan is at work in the play, and there will always be some sort of tragedy when it is acted. For this reason, some actors still refuse to use the name "Macbeth" and always refer to it as "the Scottish play".

I have a friend who, when she was young, acted in a school production of Macbeth. In one of the mock fights, using foils, the safety button came off, and one of the boys was pierced through the lung. Creepy or what? Could it have happened if the play was Romeo and Juliet?

At the same time that Shakespeare was writing, Michelangelo was painting the enormous work, the "Last Judgment" on the wall of the Sistine Chapel. It shows the joys of Heaven, but also very physical horrors of Hell.

Apart from this, there are many modern books and films about Satan, which are avidly watched and read by people who have no religion at all, and enjoy being terrified, or watching stories of innocence being defiled.

FASCINATION WITH EVIL

Why is it that so many children watched "Dr. Who" from behind the sofa, so that they could hide when it got too scary, but who would not have missed the programme for the world? Why are so many successful thrillers about the most perverted serial killers? And why are so many elderly ladies addicted to endless replays of detective stories such as Miss Marple, Hercules Poirot, Frost, Morse, Murder She Wrote, or Taggart? Be it said that murder films with overtones of supernatural evil are even more gripping, especially when backed up by shadowy figures in the dark, wearing masks, chanting, rituals in the woods, and *very* creepy music.

There are I think three major explanations:

1. One is that human beings love stories, and the devil is not only a personification of all that is evil and frightening in this world, but also a great story that gives us an adrenalin fix, and makes the real terrors of life easier to cope with.
2. Secondly, it is a projection, and enables us to think of anger, rage, lust perversion and cruelty as "out there", not part of ourselves, which would cause us great anxiety.
3. Thirdly, it helps us to cope with the splitting of our personality, when we are convinced that we did not want to do something, but that somehow, we were forced to, in spite of ourselves. "I couldn't help it, I was tempted". It is the oldest excuse in the book (see Genesis) but the reason for these acts usually lies in our own unconscious mind.

We watch terrifying programmes so that we can feel the thrill of the fear, the adrenaline rush, get rid of our own murderous thoughts and yet be comfortable in our own homes with a cup of tea or a glass of wine or beer.

GREEK TRAGEDY

The Ancient Greeks wrote tragedies, which told of murder, jealousy, rage, madness and even cannibalism. Although the horrors were not acted on the stage, but talked about by the actors, the events were horrendous. Sons murdered their parents, Mothers killed their children and then cooked and ate them, and people were driven mad by guilt or the need for revenge.

Meanwhile the Greek men watched, (no women allowed) sitting in the warm sunshine, probably with a cushion, and a flask of wine, and then went home to their wives and a supper of bread, olives, goat's cheese and more wine, and felt better for it.

The Greeks, as so often, had a word for it, *catharsis,* which meant that you felt a lot better after being terrified out of your skull and wrung with anguish and pity, facing up to the terrible horrors of this world – provided of course that you were watching all this in comfort and security.

In fact this was the method used by the psychoanalyst Freud. In a pleasant room, and lying on a comfortable couch, you could tell the therapist all the terrible traumas, anguishes and fears, which spoiled your life and turned you into nervous wreck. Over time, in the following calm, non-judgmental discussions, you began to feel better.

Being non-judgmental was a big aspect of the Greek Tragedies. It was believed that people could not help the terrible things which they did. Frequently they were driven to hideous actions by fate, or gods who were vindictive, jealous, or angry at something else. Life was simply like that and you had to accept it. The audience could only feel great pity for those doomed to such a fate.

Freud had a similar attitude. What has happened has happened, and making people feel guilty is not the way forward, but helping them to understand what is going on helps them to feel better. .

Jesus too, was always non-judgmental. When they brought before him a woman who had been taken in adultery, and they wanted to stone her to death, He simply said, "Let him who is without sin throw the first stone." And they went away, beginning with the eldest, because they were ashamed.

TERROR IS REAL

It is not only priests who may have used terror to frighten subordinates. The leadership of the Freemasons comes to mind, with the administration of blood-curdling oaths, which probably not many Englishmen take seriously these days. However there were times in the past, and no doubt still are, places where they are taken very seriously indeed.

Terror is a part of human life. Making other people terrified, even children, is still an accepted method of control, often unconscious. It is certain that those who have minds full of hatred and perversity are able to project this into the minds of others. Children who have been continuously and deliberately terrified, often go on being terrified for the rest of their lives and are easily victimised by others. They may then go on to terrorise other people.

It is easy for us to dismiss tales of demons and ghosties and things that go bump in the night. We even make a game of it on Hallowe'en, when children dress up in frightening clothes and masks - often of Devils and witches - and are rewarded with sweets and other nice things to eat. This is a means of controlling our fears. Children are too excited to be frightened, and enjoy the idea of frightening the adults.

Even so, evil is real. Terrible things do happen all the time. Some people seem to suffer far more than is their just share. The Nazi death camps come to mind. Surely, we feel, this cannot be anything other than pure evil, something out there. We find it hard to believe that human beings could create anything so horrible without prompting from some evil spirit.

Unfortunately, human beings, especially if they are psychologically damaged, can do anything nasty that they can imagine. The power of human destructive emotions, destructive to oneself, as well as others is enormous. If they were terrorised as children, people will easily and simply take to terrorising others. It is what Freud called "the return of the repressed". In Jesus' parable, the seed sown among thorns gives no harvest. In the past, vast numbers of children were terrorised without anyone thinking it was wrong. Chickens come home to roost.

Terror of demons existed long before Christianity, and it is a dark aspect of the human psyche. J.K Rowling in her non-Christian, but powerful Harry Potter novels, uses the idea of the hideous Dementors, whose kiss will suck out all love and hope and leave the victim in a state of unbearable despair forever. This is a powerful dramatisation of human terror.

The truth is that fear lies buried deep within all of us, we live on the edge of terror much of the time, and we have reason, for we must all die. All people have their own idea of hell, and some of them act it out in gruesome rituals.

One of the reasons why we read thrillers and detective stories or watch horror films, is to keep the unspeakable under control. We need to believe that, on the whole, people don't do horrible things and that if they do, there is a reason. Furthermore, Superman, Hercules Poirot, Miss Marple, Inspector Morse or Rankin's Inspector Rebus will come and sort things out. James Bond will save the world with style and panache.

But the world is a terrifying place. Apart from floods, plagues and earthquakes, armies and governments are bombing the hell out of people. Cities are destroyed, women raped, children slaughtered

To small children life can be terrifying beyond belief, today I read in my paper that in North Korea, babies born to women in prison camps are routinely killed. Closer to home, for tiny children and babies, this terror often exists within the home. Some weeks ago, my newspaper told me that thousands of children need protection from their parents. If one of these, driven beyond endurance, eventually turns on his tormentors, will he too be called a "Devil Child"?

How does the child cope with terror? By taking it to mother or father. But what if mother or father *is* the source of the terror? In an age in which parents routinely inflicted savage punishments on their children, the child was left carrying around a burden of fear, which had no relief.   The child dare not describe the father as evil, it needs the father for survival, but projects it out there, onto a cruel being, a monster, which in adult imagination becomes a demon, or devil.

If parents are cruel, children believe that it is their own fault, they deserve it. Eventually, if the child is helped by a friend or relative, to name the terror, to put it "out there" and say, "Mum and Dad shouldn't do this," there is some easing. If not, the terror is there, buried, ready to be handed out to the next generation.

Historically this applied to all grown ups. Constant fear was a harsh fact of life. It was buried deep inside us, but if it was named, then it could be talked about. It was the Devil, Satan, and the Enemy. Things could be done to prevent it - praying, being good, crossing fingers, touching wood, wearing an amulet for protection, a "miraculous medal", or wearing a lucky rabbit's foot. Such is the power of the human mind that it often seemed to work.

In the modern world, if the terror is outside us, in a book or a film, we can soothe ourselves with a cup of tea, coca cola, a glass of wine, a packet of popcorn or crisps. Small children can hide behind the sofa.

So, we project all the evil within us on to the Devil – hoofs, horns, tail and all, to make ourselves feel good and less frightened.   This is obviously a throwback to the pagan Great God Pan, half man, half goat, wildly lustful, who haunted the woods spreading Terror and Panic wherever he went.

There is in all of us, deep down, a very primitive fear and horror of total evil without boundaries. It is enhanced by the idea of darkness, perverse sexuality and disguise. The nastier newspapers exploit this to the full, writing about it and inventing every salacious detail they can imagine. They know that the perverse sexuality is exciting for a great many people, they want more, and that sells newspapers.

People with very severe emotional and mental illness (often caused by childhood suffering) really do feel that the torments within them prove that they are possessed by something evil. One reason for this is that they often hear voices in their heads.

Sometimes these voices can be kind and benign. At other times they can be vicious, cruel and sadistic and may tell the victim to do terrible things. Small wonder that the wretched victim feels persecuted by an evil spirit from outside himself. There must have been many thousands of cases like this in history. As a result we project all our evil thoughts and imaginings onto "the Devil" in order to make us feel better.

The way to fight cruelty is not with more cruelty, but with respect and love. The vision of Jesus is a vision of a world based not on hatred, fear and blame, but on Love and respect for others. He wanted all people to share in the infinite love of God. "Love one another as I have loved you."

The Holy Spirit of Christianity is described as pure Love, the Loving Spirit which permeates the Universe. Large portions of St. John's gospel are entirely about the need for love. St. James said that he who says that he loves God, but hates his brother, is deluded. St. Paul said that Love casts out fear.

The whole ethos of Christianity is about the healing power of love, but real love is hard work, as parents know. The psychoanalyst Freud, not a Christian, but an "unbelieving Jew" said that he wanted neurotic people, troubled souls, to be cured so that they could love and work.

Chapter Ten

The Origins Of Human Evil

*The fathers have eaten sour grapes and the children's
teeth are set on edge.*

Jeremiah 31.29

People quite obviously do bad things. A short list of the evils committed
by humanity in the first ten years of the twenty-first century, would take a
very long time to put together, be impossible in fact. For the truth is that
many people do very bad things to one another, all the time

We wage wars, we are greedy, rich people become even more ob-
scenely rich, and poor people become even more degradingly poor and
starving. Racism, murder and rape, continue unabated, and respectable
people make and sell horrific weapons, which enable other people to kill
one another in large numbers. Cruelty, fear, bullying and torture often
seem to be increasing. Many newspapers encourage tribal hatred, contempt for others, greed and envy because it sells more papers and they
get more money for advertising.

What then is the cause of all of this horrific behaviour?

The traditional religious explanation, based on a literal interpretation
of the Bible, is that since the disobedience of Adam, by eating the forbidden apple of the tree of knowledge, all human beings are banished

from happiness (the Garden of Eden). The story goes that happiness and innocence have gone forever, and since then humans are tormented by crude passions leading to sin and death. The clincher to this is that it was all Eve's fault, because she was led astray by the Serpent, ate the apple and then seduced Adam to do the same thing. So, for thousands of years, women were blamed for all the evils in the world. The Greeks had a similar idea with the story of Pandora's Box.

The truth is that human beings can be dreadfully aggressive, vicious, cruel, greedy and lustful. This is what the Church described as "original sin" in an effort to explain what was going on. However, Freud told us that many of these acts spring from our unconscious minds, and that we cannot stop repeating these actions, without conscious awareness of what we are doing and why.

So what is the cause of evil and hatred? Human beings do seem to be incredibly aggressive, greedy, and hungry for power over others. We have recently seen that leaving people in charge of budgets worth billions is simply an invitation to many of them to help themselves to wealth beyond the dreams of avarice, and cause a world recession.

Once Darwin published "The Origin of the Species" in 1859, it became increasingly difficult to take the Adam and Eve story literally but the early Church had never said it was the literal truth and did see the whole Adam and Eve story as a parable or allegory.

Some people say that since Darwin, evil is all about power. "All power corrupts, and absolute power corrupts absolutely," said Lord Acton. Someone else coined the phrase "might is right" about ten years after Darwin published Origin of the Species, This isn't what Darwin actually said, because what he said was that it was a matter of the survival of the fittest.

"Survival of the fittest" did not mean the biggest and strongest. In the ocean, the fittest are those who can stay underwater the longest, or swim the fastest, build outrigger canoes and navigate. In a jungle the fittest are those who are light and nimble and can easily climb trees. Everywhere, the fittest are those who can light fires at will and keep them burning, a trick learned by humans and no other animal. In all societies, those who can read, write and do arithmetic have an advantage over those who can't.

So being the fittest to survive is not about being big, strong, muscular or tough, and it does not necessarily cause evil.

Marx said that evil is caused by inequality. Under capitalism he thought, evil is inevitable. He believed that poverty and inequality are the main causes of all evil. Under an egalitarian society he thought that human evil would fade away, and he dreamed of a paradise of equality. Of course we know that in Russian and China, efforts to construct a Marxist utopian society failed dismally and totally ignored the needs and rights of the individual. The Chinese and the Russians seem to have largely given up on the idea.

Churches and religions of all sorts agree that the evil tendencies of man and woman, made worse by sin, are the main causes of evil. The Catholic Church has called this "Original Sin", and St. Augustine believed that this basic sinfulness was handed on from one generation to the next. Many people still believe that humans are tempted to do evil things by wicked spirits called devils or demons. Baptism is supposed to drive the devil out.

These are all ways of saying that "it is not my fault". They seem to have a point for even St. Paul said that he did not do what he wanted to do, and often did what he did not want to do.

HUMAN DEVELOPMENT

At the beginning of the twentieth century, Freud claimed that our actions often come from unconscious impulses deep within us. Although we may have a sophisticated intelligence, computers and civilisation - emotionally we are as primitive as our Stone Age ancestors living in caves. Since Freud, therapists, and more recently neuro-scientists, understand that emotionally, every newborn baby is basically a Stone Age baby, and has an awful lot of adapting to do, in about eighteen years.

If, in spite of dangers and difficulties, the baby is supported by sufficient, ongoing, good enough care, and if the parents or carers are able to bond sufficiently with the child in spite of their own problems and difficulties, then the child has a good chance of growing up to be a reasonably generous, good-hearted, sympathetic adult, able to make firm, long-lasting relationships and be a mature, responsible human being.

If childhood is one of neglect, harshness, loneliness, repeated vicious or cruel experience, or lack of basic sympathy, small traumas repeated over and over again with very little respite, the chances of the child growing up good, kind and mature are remote.

The harsher the childhood background, and the more continuous the trauma with very little relief, the worse all of these problems are, and the more frequently they are repeated in the next generation.

One form of trauma is for a very young boy to be sent away from home to an all-male boarding school at a very early age. The child is deprived of maternal emotional contact at a very early age, and in order to survive, develops a false exterior manner, apparently friendly, charming and co-operative, but superficial and unable to empathise with others. There is a tendency to idealise the lost mother, but also to conceal anger with women because of the abandonment. This is the cause of much misogyny. The younger the child, the worse and more long-lasting is the damage. This is now known as Boarding School Syndrome.

It is worth considering that many, if not most of the Church theologians in the past were raised in boarding schools, junior seminaries or monasteries. There was a very high level of physical punishment in all of these places. A current member of the British government is frequently referred to as "Thrasher" because of the beatings he inflicted on younger boys at Eton. Church boarding schools too were also well known for their harsh "discipline". This would have been made worse by telling the boys that all of this was the will of God. It is no wonder that many older priests have huge emotional problems.

In the worst possible cases of neglect and abuse, the result is a miserable and unhappy, mentally disturbed, maladjusted and possibly criminal man or woman.

Freud finally got rid of human guilt by saying that we do not always have free will in these matters, but are often guided by the unconscious. Apparently this is now borne out by neuro-science, which has been able to detect electric activity in the relevant part of the brain, *before* people have consciously thought of some specific action.

Jesus had what seem like very simple answers to all of this – even if we have to prevent people doing evil, we must not hate them. Love one another, forgive one another unto seventy times seven, turn the other cheek, and accept children (they are so childish). If a man steals your shirt give it to him and your cloak also. Judge not lest you shall be judged; remove the beam of wood from your own eye before you tell your neighbour to remove the splinter from his. Blessed are the poor, blessed are the merciful, love one another as I have loved you, love your neighbour, whoever he is.

Why, with all of this, and the firm belief that Jesus came to take away our sins, are so many sermons, homilies and religious writings about sin? Why do we rush to condemn so many human actions as sinful? It is because in order to survive mentally and emotionally in a judgmental society, human beings need to see themselves as good and therefore others as evil.

To know or believe that we are bad is unbearable, this is the fruit of the tree of knowledge of good and evil, so we often split and project all of our unworthiness on to others. We are good they are bad. They are so bad that they deserve eternal punishment, or at least lock them up and throw away the key.

The word "atonement" in early English meant "at-one-ment" something which makes us all "at one" with each other and "at one" with God, instead of thousands of separate little fighting egos and tribes. We humans are so devious and manipulative however, that the word has completely lost its original meaning and now means suffering, doing penance, begging for forgiveness. It is as if we have given up on unity.

Why is it that men beat not only their enemies, but their wives and children also? In theory we have been trying Christianity for two thousand years, but with two world wars in the last century, the Holocaust, and constant hideous wars since, we don't seem to doing very well. The answer lies in repression of our own unconscious anger and rage.

Freud came up with a grand theory of mental illness being caused by repressed sexuality. Many of his followers now know that there is much more to it than this, but he said it only after listening to dozens of patients, many of whom were women, and they told him that they knew what had caused their problems – abuse, much of it sexual. Unlike many men, he listened; he believed them and thought seriously about what they said. Hundreds – no, thousands of his followers have done the same, and a large body of evidence is building up about the causes of evil, and why so many human beings are just so plain cussed and nasty.

Freud's most famous contribution to solving some of these problems was to *listen to what people said,* and by people he very definitely included women and children, even very small children. In one or two of his earliest cases he listened to what people had said to others. A friend of his, who was a doctor, had a patient, a woman who had a great many symptoms, which we would call hysterical. Now Freud had studied hysteria in Paris, and he seems to have been one of the first people to realise that you did not just *do things* to these sick people (hypnosis was favourite then, though drugs are generally administered now) but you also listened to what they had to say.

Many of Freud's early women clients in Vienna said that they had been sexually abused as children and young women. In fact we now know that sexual abuse in families is far more widespread than anyone could have imagined in the days when we didn't talk about it. It happens frequently and always has the most dreadful effects on those who were victims, creating great unhappiness and severe mental instability in the worst cases. The English writer Virginia Woolf, who finally committed suicide was a case in point

A hundred years ago, most Europeans, religious and atheist alike, would have said that children soon forget, and cannot be permanently harmed by such things. The problem is that children blame themselves, and feel guilty, as well as feeling totally worthless. These feelings may never go away.

It seems that many elderly men, including cardinals and bishops, lawyers and judges, all trained to think logically, still think that children forget. However, the memory of the trauma, even if consciously forgotten, is buried deep in the unconscious, is repressed and causes mental and emotional suffering in the victim, all the more vicious because it is hidden. Often this causes terrible mental illness and even perversion.

When I was a young teacher, it was still believed that a child living with an abusive family was better off with that family than with strangers. In my first school, a little boy and his even smaller sister, aged four, both known to be regularly abused, were left by the authorities in a horrific situation. I often grieve and wonder what happened to them.

At first, Freud believed that sexual child abuse caused enormous harm, and began to lecture and write on the topic. Trouble ensued. Not only did people not believe him (this was the nineteenth century) but the scientific societies, which he addressed, actively opposed him. He ran into so much public opposition from other medical men that he began to doubt his own thought processes. Certainly it became obvious that the more he pursued this, the more opposition he ran into.

Finally, Freud doubted himself, and could not believe that so many of those respectable Viennese men had been abusing their daughters and relatives. He decided that many of these cases (though not all) were imagined, or desired, and then repressed. He was wrong.

The original basic discovery was, that what happens in childhood affects us as we grow up. If a girl has a good enough relationship with her father, and a boy with his mother, then they are able to mature properly. What causes the problem is not only external events, but the relationship between the child and the parents.

What has become even more obvious in the last century is that severe unhappiness in a child, because of loss, neglect, or vicious, perverse and cruel experience, will result in a severely unhappy and maladjusted adult. After so many wars in the twentieth century, and ongoing in the twenty-first, millions of children were abandoned or neglected, and led unhappy damaged lives, and this would affect *their children* in many unfortunate ways.

Hitler caused orphanages to be built. Outstandingly "Aryan" soldiers and women (tall and blonde) met in luxurious circumstances with the express aim of conceiving children. The father went back to wherever he had come from, and was never heard of again. As soon as the child was born it was taken away from the mother, and the tall blonde children were raised in orphanages – probably like boarding schools, and these were intended to be the heroic Nazis of the future, fit, hard, emotionless.

When these places were found, after the war, the unfortunate children were found to be backward and underdeveloped emotionally and intellectually.

It is no accident that many of the traditional fairy tales, stories of survival for children, begin with the child losing or being abandoned by parents.

CRIMINAL BEHAVIOUR

The German author Alice Miller, was convinced that cruelty or harshness towards children causes more cruelty and harshness in the next generation. She was not well known, because people simply do not want to believe this. She was convinced that the cruelty and harshness of child rearing in German Prussia was the main cause of Germany's need to declare war in Europe twice in the twentieth century. One might say that some similar situation caused the empire building of the British in the nineteenth and early twentieth centuries. A friend tells me that her husband, as a boy at school, would be beaten by a teacher and then be obliged to thank the teacher and shake hands with him. Repressed anger and frustration must have been enormous.

Military generals on both sides in the First World War were products of harsh boarding school Victorian upbringing, became dissociated from their own painful feelings and so were able to endure without suffering the fact that they were sending hundreds of thousands of healthy young men to their deaths every day.

Miller makes the point about Adolf Hitler who caused more suffering and death in the twentieth century than any man, with the possible exception of Stalin. Hitler's father was a harsh and violent man. His mother had lost five children through miscarriage and sickness before Adolf was born. With a life like that and a harsh husband, she must have been sunk in misery and depression before her son was born. He was certainly, as far as we know, cared for physically, for unlike the others he survived. Then an aunt, who was completely crazy was brought to live in the household. It must have been horrific.

It is no wonder that when he got power, one of Hitler's first acts was to destroy the insane. Hitler was beaten savagely and for long periods of time by his father, and one of his proud boasts was that he did not cry. It is said that as an adult the only relationship Hitler could sustain with a woman was perverse. Normal human relationships were impossible for him.

He became a complete narcissist. What this means is that he was totally dissociated from any feeling about pain. He became a psychopath, and had no feelings about human suffering whatever. Because he was without conscience, he became charming, friendly, and able to attract people.

Hitler was utterly ruthless, cruel, selfish, manipulative, power-mad and vicious. In spite of this, aided by right-wing German politicians who thought that they could control him, he was able to take over power and act out these terrible aspects of his character, aided by people like him, and millions died all over Europe.

Millions of Jews, Poles, Russians, gypsies, and mentally and physically handicapped people were slaughtered without mercy, because Hitler needed to prove that he was better than others. In this he was backed up by the tribal feelings of national rivalry across Europe. For many years after Hitler's death, Europeans suffered destruction, hunger, homelessness, poverty, sickness and disruption

So was it Hitler's fault? Yes. Could he help it? No, he couldn't help himself. With no one to control him, there was nothing else he could do. He was raised with harsh violence, depression and insanity, and worst of all he was raised without love. Even worse, there were enough damaged people in Germany like him, some of them powerful and wealthy and urging him on.

Hitler was able to do all of these things, because he was hated as a child. And why did millions of people allow him to do it? Because they had not been loved for themselves either, but trained, often trained in a military style of harshness and cruelty. Alice Miller's books have much to say about child rearing in Germany before World War II. But it was the same all over Europe. As King George V of England is reputed to have said,

"I was afraid of my father, and by God, my children will be afraid of me."

His eldest son, Edward, abdicated the throne to be with an older woman, (a kinder mother figure?) and his younger son suffered from a lifelong and debilitating stutter. For both of them, a happy marriage seems to have brought some sort of redemption.

People were trained to become hard working, disciplined, obedient to death, loyal, good fathers and providers. But often they were not taught the most important lesson of all – love, compassion, kindness, respect pity and goodwill to all, and they were not taught it because many of their parents didn't know how. They could not love others because they could not love themselves, and they could not love themselves because *their* parents had been unable to show them much love. You cannot teach love by teaching; you can only teach love by loving kindness. Jesus was literally right. So was Freud, who believed that the close relationship between therapist and client could help people to lead useful lives of work and love.

THE HISTORY OF CHILDHOOD

If anyone wishes to explore some of the extraordinary ways in which children have been treated in Europe over the last thousand years or so, they can do no better than read a *History of Childhood*, edited by Lloyd de Mause. Childhood in many cases meant laborious toil, slavery, hunger, humiliation, prostitution and even castration, organised by adults. It is a big book, but all of the information is taken from the writings of people who were alive when these things happened, and they did not necessarily think of them as wrong.

As we well know, these things are still happening now, across the world. People survive as best they can. In the seventeenth, eighteenth and even early nineteenth centuries, deliberate castration before puberty of thousands of choirboys was common in Europe, and especially in Italy. This was so that men could sing powerful alto and soprano women's parts in the cathedrals and opera houses of Europe. A few of these boys became the pop stars of their age making fortunes, but it must be emphasised that most did not. Hoping to make money, many were castrated by their own families, and many died. Even the choir of the Vatican Sistine

Chapel had some of these "castrati singers" though there was a great deal of opposition.

Before we say that children were always treated kindly here in England, let us remember the little boys sent up chimneys to clean them, and the fires lit under their feet so that they would wriggle if they got stuck. There were little girl "slavvies" scrubbing and cleaning in the households of the middle classes, there were children who spent hours throwing stones at crows or opening and closing ventilation traps in the dark in mines. Many children worked for very long hours in the cotton mills, cleaning up and inhaling the dust and fluff under the machines, in danger of horrific accidents, while they were still working. Remember the savage beatings and bullying for the children of the rich in the English "Public" schools.

Remember too, that in the past, the eldest boys of royalty, who were to rule nations, hardly ever saw their parents. Even middle class people often sent their sons away from home to be reared by others, farmed out, or sent to boarding schools. Illegitimate children were often hidden in this way. Cruelty is often not a deliberate act of will, but an unconscious "acting out" by those whose lives have suffered trauma since they were small – it did me no harm. .

In America, the fundamental vicious sadism of the Rifle Association, is expressed in their refusal to ban easy access to guns of all sorts, no matter how many American children are killed. Because of their own up-bringing, there is huge dissociation of intellect from feelings. Their mantra is that it is not guns that kill but people.

This is absolutely true, but the fact is that so many people are seriously disturbed, not to say crazy, that guns and people should be kept as far apart from one another as possible. Every human being is capable of murder when it is so easy. It is always childhood suffering, neglect and abandonment, which causes violence and cruelty in adult humans

In case any one thinks that this is a sweetly pretty idea, pie in the sky, something invented by counsellors to obtain well paying clients, it is worth repeating that all of this is now backed up by modern technology in the form of neuro-science.

Studies of the brain and the chemicals in it show that children who have lost their parents, are never shown affection, or have mothers suffering from post-natal depression, without support, have the chemical composition of their brains altered, totally lacking in dopamine or serotonin, natural opiates, which make us feel secure and content and give us strength and motivation. During the rest of their lives they may suffer from depression, or illness - their brains permanently flooded by cortisol, another hormone, caused by, and resulting in, constant misery. This clearly set out in Sue Gerhardt's book *Why Love matters.*

Human evil is not caused by devils, demons, or DNA but by childhood suffering. This is the original sin, not mystic evil passed on by sex. Unfortunately the Church in the past, like many human institutions, has too often been seen as a critical and punitive parent, rather than a loving and nurturing parent. Evangelisation must begin here. If we do not feel loved by the Church, which we can see, how can we feel loved by God, who we don't see?

Chapter Eleven

The Seven Deadly Sins

The "seven deadly sins" sounds like the title of a lurid film. I fact, I'm pretty sure it was the title of film, probably in the old black and white days. It sounds exciting, evil and seductive at the same time, because, frankly, we are quite attracted to the idea of behaving badly, and by watching a film, we can do it by proxy.

But why deadly? And why seven?

MYSTICAL SEVEN

For thousands of years, all mathematicians in Europe and Asia firmly believed that numbers were not merely for counting the goats, the bushels of wheat or the money. There was something much more mystical, almost magical, about numbers and the number seven was traditionally held to be perfect and complete. This may be because the week, a quarter of a lunar month, is exactly seven days, and it may also be because it seems that seven is the number of things most people can remember easily, give or take one or two.

According to the first book of the Bible, even God respected the number seven by making the universe in six days, and resting on the seventh. When the disciples asked if they should forgive their enemies seven times before giving up on them, Jesus replied that they should forgive people "seventy times seven", meaning infinity.

Because of the power of seven it was probably felt that in making lists, you were bound to have covered all the main points. So in Catholic theology there are quite a few lists with exactly seven items in each. There are seven sacraments, seven corporal works of mercy, seven spiritual works of mercy, the seven gifts of the Holy Spirit, and of course, the Seven Deadly Sins.

Given this emotional need at the time to put everything into lists of seven, it is not surprising that sin, the dark side of humanity, should also have its list of seven. There have been different lists over the centuries and in the fourteenth century, many European painters, such as Hieronymus Bosch created great works of art based on those human evils.

The definitive list seems to be as follows: Wrath, Greed, Sloth, Lust, Envy, Gluttony and Pride. Whenever I try to remember the list, sloth, or laziness is the one I invariably forget, probably because it is the one I feel most prone to (my unconscious at work again). These sins were called "deadly" because they were believed to kill the soul, to destroy our humanity, and send people to hell for eternity.

People believed this list to be definitive, accurate, and logical but we now have a different way of looking at bad behaviour. If, as I have tried to suggest, we think that psychology tells us more about human behaviour than philosophy and logic, then evil or self destructive behaviour must be considered as an emotional illness, rather than a deliberate evil act of will.

BRAIN ACTIVITY

Though our brains may look dull and grey, we now know that they are powerhouses of enormous electrical activity greater than that of a computer. It is vitally important however, to realise that our brains respond not only to intellectual activity, but *also to emotional activity.* If we recite our "times table" there is brain activity, but if we laugh, our grey cells are also busy signalling one another. If we weep, electric messages again run races around the brain.

It has recently been established that reading a novel gives far more exercise to the brain than solving a crossword puzzle. In reading a novel the brain is far more engaged at all sorts of different levels, emotional as well as intellectual. Because of the emotional connection, we keep on thinking about a novel for a long time, which we do not do with ordinary puzzles.

Because of the modern study of neuroscience, and the ability to scan the brain, we now have actual scanned images of the brains of children who have been well cared for. We also have images of the brains of children who have been neglected, abused, tormented and battered. The grey matter, the "little grey cells" of well cared for children are plump and normal. In contrast, the brains of abused children are shrunken and shrivelled; they take up less space, and are obviously *physically damaged*.

Not only this, but the actual chemical composition of a child's brain is irrevocably altered for the worse when the child receives continual ill-treatment, so that emotional and intellectual activity are crippled for life.

It seems that there are three main chemicals or hormones, which affect brain activity, and these chemicals, are affected by what happens to someone. These are: Dopamine, Serotonin and Cortisol. In a normal personality these hormones are probably well balanced. (See Sue Gerhardt *Why Love Matters*)

Dopamine and serotonin are what are known as opioids. Their existence in the brain makes the individual more upbeat, capable and active. If there is love, security, affection and happy experience, then dopamine and serotonin flood the brain and reinforce the happy experience. If the child is belittled, abused, or faced with constant change and loss, tormented or seriously neglected, then not only do the opioids disappear, but they are replaced by cortisol, which reinforces misery and unhappiness.

There are also endorphins and these also make us feel better, but they are brought into action by human activity, exercise or sport. Children who are kept immobile, such as the Romanian orphans who for years were kept in cots all day, would never experience the good effects of activity. With reference to the Romanian orphans, apparently those who were rescued before the age of four had the best chance of adaptation to ordinary life.

Repetitions of happy and affectionate experiences fix the amount of dopamine and serotonin, which become steady, and help to balance and develop the child's personality. If, on the other hand, there is a constant repetition of unhappy or punitive experiences such as loss, trauma or terror, then cortisol takes over more or less permanently, and a very unbalanced unhappy personality is the result.

The manifestations of such a personality are reflected in the "Seven Deadly Sins."

ANGER

Children are usually forbidden by the parent to be angry, (this is naughty behaviour) and must repress the anger or receive even more punishment and humiliation. Repressed anger can have many terrible results, including lifelong depression.

There have been several books lately, notably by Nick Duffel and Joy Shaverein, about the emotional damage done to children who are sent away from their families to be raised in boarding schools. .It is worth remembering that in his autobiography, C.S. Lewis gave the name "Belsen" to the prep school to which he and his brother were sent.

If children are sent away before they are ten years old, they may never fully mature. This may say a great deal about the junior seminaries to which many boys were sent in the past. The total deprivation of family affection is made worse by the institutional fear of homosexuality. According to Freud's theory of "the return of the repressed," the original feelings will burst out in the adult in all sorts of ways, and at all sorts of inappropriate times. Trying to control anger, without finding the original cause, may be like sticking a plaster on a volcano,

The man or woman who has been treated harshly as a child and represses the fact, will treat others harshly, and may take it out on his students, or his family. If he is so ill that he is psychotic, he may become powerful through bullying and manipulation, and may, like Hitler, Stalin, Pol Pot and countless others, destroy millions.

It may seem simplistic, but it is true nevertheless, that militaristic leaders and politicians who glorify war, and drag their people into war, are mostly acting out their own childhood loss and humiliations. They have an unconscious compulsion to forget that they were once helpless, and as adults need to demonstrate their power. They are determined to revenge themselves upon their tormentors and prove their own superiority by grasping as much power over others as possible. There is never enough.

In their desperate efforts to survive, they become highly manipulative.

Autocratic rulers everywhere are reacting to their own childhood sense of helplessness. In many institutions it is a joke to say that the lunatics are running the asylum, but this may not be far from the truth. In some unfortunate and frightened souls, anger will be turned upon the self, and may result in depression, so that they are always mysteriously failing or committing self-harm, such as cutting oneself, or even suicide.

Each person is different and there are no simple solutions. True democracy may do something to prevent the crazy behaviour of emotionally damaged leaders but there were have been many such rulers in the past and still are.

Unfortunately many modern autocrats have the backing of unscrupulous financiers with their own rage and anger, who control the press the media or the arms industries, and manipulate these damaged people to carry out their own agendas of grasping power at all costs.

GREED

Greed affects people who as children never, ever had enough love or care.

In recent years there has been a general monetary collapse across the globe, a "credit crunch". Although politicians have been quick to blame one another, it is clear that this was caused by investment banks and so called "hedge funds", which "hedge their bets" by gambling with vast amounts of other people's money, and losing astronomical sums.

Obviously this was about greed, which humans are particularly prone to. But what is it that makes people so greedy that they risk everything (many bankers lost their well paid jobs) in the hope of creating vast and unsustainable profits? The Devil? Original sin?

Well no. The psychological consensus is that greed is caused by emotional deprivation or dire poverty early in life. There may be many causes for this, including illness, loss of a parent, or seeing little of one's parents, and being sent away to boarding schools at a very early age. Boarding schools often give a misplaced sense of entitlement.

The greater the deprivation of love and affection when they were small, the more people will desperately try to fill the emotional space with other things, such as money, and at the same time, deny their loss. Depending on your opportunities and inclinations, you may collect piles of old newspapers, more books than you can possibly read, many lovers, as much money as you can get away with, or maybe all of these things including actually owning newspapers.

An example from my own early experience is that of a deputy head of a school, with a very large workload. She was a married woman, but having no children of her own, had adopted two young children, a boy and a girl, who attended the school where she worked.

Unfortunately, at morning break, the little boy not only had his own sixpence to spend on biscuits, but would invariably steal another sixpence or whatever he could lay his hands on. Every time he was always found out. His mother was deeply distressed, and on one occasion, finally driven beyond endurance, was seen raging, dragging the little boy through the school.

There you are, theft, greed and dishonesty, bred in the bone. Did he have evil parents? Or what was it? Bad blood? Original sin? However, the little boy's problem was not about honesty, but emotional deprivation, a lack of love.

He had lost his own mother. Although he saw his adopted mother every day in school she was not with him, but busy looking after other children. In the evening I am sure she loved him and spent time with him, but also she had a lot of preparation to do, and as he was only six, I imagine he went to bed early.

Saturday must have been a busy day, cleaning and shopping (no open shops on Sunday in those days, nor late into the evening) and that left Sunday. His mother was a good church-going woman and played the organ at least twice and often more frequently at different churches, taking the children with her.

The little boy simply did not feel that he had enough of his adopted mother's attention, and he lacked emotional security. She loved him dearly, but she could not show it, and he could not feel it. Stealing was his way of attracting his mother's attention at break. She was angry and upset, but any attention was better than none.

Am I saying that all of these people who have wrecked the economy, by gambling with our money, are poor little children who should be forgiven? Well, like most people, I have a feeling that they should all be strung up. But this is my anger speaking. There is obviously something wrong with a system where people give their money to bankers who not only squander it, but then give themselves big rewards for doing so.

GLUTTONY

Although it used to be said that fat people are jolly people, most people now know that overeating and being overweight are closely allied to depression. Overeating makes you put on weight, being overweight develops illnesses and makes you feel bad about yourself, and so you eat (or drink) some more and put on more weight and feel worse. The emotionally deprived child (and adult) has an unconscious empty emotional space within, which they often try to fill with comfort eating.

Were Thomas Aquinas and other philosophers right then in saying that we have powerful passions, which must be kept under control? Yes, but control is not a matter of will power, which has severe limits. Nor is it a matter of a knowledge of philosophy but help by caring adults. Many people are depressed and overweight because their parents were depressed and overweight and fed them all the wrong foods. One of the big questions of children and adults who are overweight is, who is feeding them?

There is a persistent legend that St. Thomas Aquinas was himself extremely overweight, so overweight, was the malicious story, that he had to have a curve cut out of the dining table so that he could reach the food. As he wrote a book called the *Summa Theologica* – the *Total of All Theology* - there is also an English joke that when he was rebuked for his excess weight, he replied that "it takes more than one swallow to make a Summa".... sorry about that.

Perhaps this man who devoted his life to reason and logic may also have been emotionally deprived as a child and tried to make up for it in the usual way.

SLOTH

It is often said that the normal human response to danger is flight or fight. This is only partly true however, for there is a third possible reaction, caused by such terrified fright, that the sufferer freezes like a rabbit caught in headlights.

Faced with ongoing fear or anxiety or conflict, the victim may be totally unable to take any action at all. I remember a case study of a young woman who had all her life been over-controlled by her mother. She was in a bad way when she met a young man with whom she fell in love and they married. Part of the wonder of this was that as they bought and furnished their house, before the wedding, the young woman, for the first time in her life, had been able to arrange things just as she wanted them.

When they came back from the honeymoon, happy and laughing, they went into the house, only find that her mother had used her key to enter the house and totally rearrange all of the furniture to suit *her* taste. The young woman collapsed, curled up into a foetal position, which she kept for weeks, and had to be taken away to a mental hospital.

Confronted with situations which bring back a fearful previous experience of total helplessness in the face of danger, some people simply refuse to move, or to get out of bed. I have heard this described as "frozen anger". In a way, this too is a form of flight, escaping from the realities of the situation.

Doctors first became aware of this during the First World War when many soldiers were so traumatised by bombs, guns, dead bodies, body parts and deadly, deep pools of mud, that they refused to move, and sometimes could not even talk. This was the first time ever that such behaviour was recognised as illness, rather than cowardice, and was called Shell Shock. Pat Barker's magnificent novel *Regeneration* illustrates this brilliantly.

LUST

Lust is sex gone wrong. Promiscuous sex is an unsatisfactory substitute for real love, and promiscuous lovers are deeply immature and unable to form stable relationships. They constantly move from one unsatisfactory affair to another, desperately looking for the stable relationship of care which they did not receive as children.

Lust causes its own difficulties for a clergy which is compulsorily celibate. In the same way that the poor are always anxious about money, so the celibate, especially if the celibacy is compulsory rather than chosen, must have far more anxieties about sex, probably unconscious, leading to either distaste or idealisation - maybe both in the same person. This completely blocks much reasonable theological discussion on the topic.

Unfortunately the Church has always seen ordinary sexual activity as "imperfect" (if celibacy is "a state of perfection" this implies that all sexual activity is "imperfect") and outside marriage any sexual activity has always been regarded as "mortally" sinful, bringing death to the soul. It is worth remembering that Jesus once said that the tax collectors and harlots would enter the Kingdom of Heaven before the perfectionist Pharisees.

As a young woman teaching in a convent boarding school, before television was universal, it was my job to show the Saturday evening film to the boarders. Every time we came to a loving embrace (and the films were really, really harmless) I was told to switch off the lamp and leave the film running until we were safely past the scene of danger. Who was this protecting, the nuns or the girls? And protecting them from what? Ordinary human relationships?   I am quite certain that the break in the picture can only serve to have highlighted for the students a problem which they didn't realise existed, thus totally defeating the object of the exercise.

If a child has been badly damaged emotionally, neglected or ignored, he or she may never be able to make real loving relationships in adult life. As an adult, such a person may desperately chase after casual sex and pornography, or even paedophilia, seeing another child as a suitable sexual partner, instead of a strong and loving bond with another adult.

ENVY

Envy of a neurotic nature also has its origins in emotional deprivation. One of Freud's followers was Melanie Klein, a therapist who specialised in studies of infancy and who was very influential in England. She saw envy as innate, something we are born with. The ordinary "good enough mother", or caregiver, can cope with this and relieve the child's anxieties. However, if the child's emotional deprivation is extreme and without relief, overwhelming envy and jealousy may become a terrible handicap in life, and a source of misery to themselves and others.

Constant envy and jealousy in adults, no matter what it seems, is not only about "the here and now" but a revival of the emotional, or physical deprivation, of the past. It seems to many lay people that the Church's constant monitoring of the sexual activity of the faithful, or the would-be priest, is probably based on unconscious envy of those for whom celibacy was not really a free choice, but an obligatory condition of their chosen vocation.

And finally -

PRIDE

This was always considered to be the greatest sin of all; the sin of Lucifer, the angel who proudly declared, "I will not serve" and the subject of countless sermons in the past. As a young nun I sat through so many sermons from priests, telling me not to be proud, that I developed a great deal of sympathy for Charles Dickens' character, Uriah Heep, with his constant repetition of the words:

"I'm ever so 'umble, Master Copperfield"

As a "charity boy" Uriah had also been obliged to listen to many sermons on the topic.

Extreme pride is often the manifestation of a narcissistic disorder. It often goes along with an intense arrogance and, oddly enough, frequently a charming, manipulative personality.

Narcissism is the result of intense childhood suffering, emotional abandonment, often caused by being sent away from their family, and to which no reaction was acceptable. So great was the unhappiness, that the child dissociates entirely from his or her feelings, because they are too painful. This is why arrogant people can be so cold, so distant, but at the same time charming (desperately trying to attract others) and extremely manipulative. This of course, can only be healed by a long term, steady loving relationship. Jane Austen was spot on with her description of Mr. Darcy.

Having no insight into their own childhood sufferings, the true narcissist can have little or no sympathy for others. Children raised in an environment without any warmth or affection and who suffer from great emotional neglect, have enormous problems, which they pass on to others. If these sad narcissistic personalities become deeply psychotic, they can cause great suffering to all of those with whom they come into contact.

So there we are. These seven deadly sins are not deliberate offences against God, they are emotional illnesses caused by emotional deprivation. Most religious people know this today as much as anyone else. But religious textbooks are often far behind, still talking in terms of strict morality and sinfulness, often presented in philosophical terms.

Alice Miller, a great writer on the sufferings of children, has much to say in her books of the cruelty, harshness and intense control of child-raising in the nineteenth and early twentieth century Germany. She is convinced, rightly so, that the harshness of the Prussian child rearing traditions, contributed much to the cruel culture of the Kaiser's Germany, and the rise of the Nazis, which otherwise seems inexplicable.

The Kaiser himself of course, suffered greatly from his mother's utter rejection of his own physical handicap, a severely damaged arm, exacerbated by his left-handedness, which was totally unacceptable at the time. The cruel "medical interventions" of the time, caused him untold suffering.

And what of England? We have more children in prison than any other country in Europe and the government refuses to outlaw smacking for small children. Why? Because the ruling classes of England for centuries have been sent away from home since their earliest years, to "public schools" where bullying and beating were regarded as normal, and the only way to train boys to become "manly".

In the past young Catholic boys were sent to similar institutions, junior seminaries, where they too were separated from family affections and surrounded by other frightened lonely boys. They then had to develop a hard emotional shell, disguised because of the obligation of charity. As in other boarding schools this was made more confusing because of the fear of homosexuality.

Years of therapeutic experience show that if there is not "good enough" physical and emotional care in childhood, the results are greed, gluttony, sloth, envy, lust, anger and pride, among other things... The full extent of the child's hidden rage depends on the degree of harshness or neglect people suffered as children.

The Church urgently needs to adopt a new approach to the theology of sin and many Catholics are aware of this. People need to be offered hope, and resurrection, not punishment or threats of eternal damnation. This hope needs to be based on Jesus' teaching and example about kindness, compassion, generosity, empathy for the suffering and poor, and forgiveness up to seventy times seven.

Chapter Twelve

The Penny Catechism

The "Penny Catechism", or Catechism of Christian Doctrine, to give it its full title, was the basis of Catholic understanding for most adults of my generation. It was the one booklet which every Catholic child read at school. We learned it off by heart, recited it at the beginning of many religious lessons and in previous generations, children were punished if they did not know the answers. Many, if not most of the elderly men running the Church must have begun their theological studies in this way, at an earlier age.

The Penny Catechism contained the teaching of the Church in microcosm, and it was meant to be the basis of our replies to those who challenged our faith. The Church has long replaced it with a modern expanded adult catechisms meant mostly for the use of priests and teachers - the last one I saw was the size of a small encyclopaedia.

Many older Catholics are aghast at the fact that Catholic schools no longer insist that the old catechism is learned by heart. Some see this as the cause of the current disintegration of the Church, and blame it for the lapse of younger Catholics and the shortage of priests. They are oblivious to the fact that many people are equally horrified and deeply disillusioned by the revelation of priestly child abuse, weary of Vatican bans on birth control, and negative obsession with sex. People want the Church to stay out of the bedroom. As it doesn't, many have left.

For some reason, I was never very good at learning the catechism, probably for the same reason that I could never remember my times' tables, it simply failed to keep my interest. In the same way that I could never see that I needed to know what eight times nine were, I didn't disagree with the catechism, couldn't argue with it, just couldn't bring myself to concentrate on it. Considering that I read everything else I could lay my hands on with avidity, could recite poems and remember stories, we have to say that to some extent, in my case at least, the Penny Catechism failed in its purpose.

Or maybe not. One of the things from it I can remember, are the "Seven Corporal Works of Mercy", because that bit did interest me; "to feed the hungry, give drink to the thirsty, to visit the sick, to visit the imprisoned, to harbour the harbourless, and to bury the dead", which seems to me unimpeachable, though I never thought that giving food to the hungry would apply to my own country, as it does now. I also realise that other Christian denominations have similar lists, probably all religions do.

On the other hand, such questions as "What considerations concerning God will lead to sorrow for our sins?" seemed to me a bit on the morbid side, similarly the instruction that when I went to bed I was to "observe modesty, occupy myself with thoughts of death and endeavour to compose myself to rest at the foot of the cross." There was obviously anxiety about sex here. That this sort of thing could be thought of as ghoulish, and lead to childish fear, was not even remotely understood. In fact, in previous generations, it might have been thought a good thing if children were afraid.

Looking at the text of the catechism now, it seems that the writers were suffering from the problems I have mentioned elsewhere. In spite of its many just observations about love of God, justice, honesty, generosity and forgiveness there was a severe splitting between feelings and intellect, and also between the ideas of body and soul.

I was about to say that no-one could accuse the catechism of appealing to the powers of the imagination, but by the previous reference to going to sleep at the foot of the cross, it was arousing guilt. Furthermore, although not stated, there were strong implications that the body is the home of the passions (and therefore inferior) while the soul, or spirit, consists of the intellect, and is therefore superior. The other powerful element is the emphasis on Augustine's bleak, pessimistic doctrine of the guilt of Original Sin as handed down from one generation to the next.

Question twenty-nine asked if there is any likeness to God in my soul. The answer was, "There is this likeness to the Blessed Trinity in my soul, that as in one God there are three Persons, so in my soul there are three powers." In this rather odd answer, the likeness to God seems to depend entirely on arithmetic. Furthermore, the three divine powers of the soul are Memory, Understanding and Will, which is a fairly limited and intellectual view of humanity – no mention of love, creativity, empathy or the indwelling of the Holy Spirit. If my memory is poor, my understanding limited and my will power not very strong, what happens to my likeness to God?

This idea of the soul has been strong in the Church because of the prayer of St. Ignatius, widely known.

> "Take O Lord, and accept all that I am,
> My memory my understanding and my will."

If Ignatius totally ignored the body in this list, this can only be that for the Church, the passions, the emotions, the feelings, are not seen as part of the soul at all, but belong only to the inferior body. In this way of looking at things, the soul is, in a strange way, seen as soulless, it has a memory, an understanding and a will, but like a robot or a computer, it has no feelings at all. I find this strange, because Ignatius' method of praying consisted of powerful visual imagination and emotional, devotional visualisation.

For Christians, the central teaching is that God is love, "Since God has loved us, we too must love one another," says St. John in his first letter. But the relationship of God and human beings in the Catechism, is seen as a religious duty, in order to "save my soul". It is intellectual rather than emotional. The feeling is that of dutifully going to see a rich relative once a week to make sure that he doesn't leave me out of his will.

The wooden question and answer system, with all the imagination and literary grace of a brick wall, was not fit for purpose. The catechism was simply not up to the task of teaching small children what it means to be a Christian, because the men who wrote it were not even remotely interested in children and their genuine needs, desires and anxieties. The 1997 edition of this catechism told us that faced with illness, sickness or pain we should say, "Lord, your will be done, I take this for my sins," which didn't really seem to have much to do with the Good News of the Gospel. Much of this was based on St. Augustine's personal pessimism about sinful humanity.

Like the times' table the catechism was built on the idea of absolute, rigorous certainty. It revealed a tendency to make religion like science, with fixed watertight answers, which left no space for thinking or feeling. It would certainly give comfort to those anxious souls who have a deep psychological need for definitive answers to any problem life might throw at them.

The Church has tried to make its teachings have the certainty of science, so that there can be no possible errors, because, as faith was seen as intellectual the really important thing was to have "right belief. "Error", or mistaken belief, was seen as the one great terrible mistake from which all sins flow, so a Pope could say "error has no rights". But this belief was intellectual belief.

The Church's trust that if you have correct intellectual belief, all the rest will follow, seems to me a bit like the government's belief that if rich people are allowed to get richer, the "trickle down" theory means that everyone else will benefit. It doesn't, and they don't. Theology, known as the "Sacred Science" came to be seen as the absolute knowledge of all things religious, the answer to all questions, but faith is not about intellect.

AN UNCERTAIN WORLD

Scientists themselves are beginning to realise that science is not nearly so scientific, not nearly absolute, as they once thought. It used to be believed, for example, that with modern methods, weather could be accurately predicted for six months or so ahead. Harsh experience has shown that this simply isn't so.

In England many of us still treasure the memory from 1987, of Michael Fish, a much respected meteorologist, telling us on television, with absolute confidence that it was certainly not true that a hurricane would soon hit England. He told us we had nothing to worry about, and that it was certain the winds would go south and hit Spain instead. This happened about twelve hours before we had the greatest storm to hit England in three hundred years. It killed nineteen people and tore up thousands of trees, leaving many blocked roads, whole areas without electricity and long term devastation.

Eventually the weathermen gave up making long-term forecasts, because they realised that anything can happen, and the whole thing was too uncertain. This is partly based on the new scientific Chaos Theory.

Anything can happen, we simply don't know. This theory is summed up by saying that if a butterfly flaps its wings in Florida, it could eventually result in a tornado in Kansas.

AN UNCERTAIN WORLD

Scientists are now realising that many "absolute facts" including "scientific predictions" about the stock exchange or the economy, are not half as absolute as they were once thought to be. For instance, it was once believed to be an absolute, unalterable scientific fact that Halley's Comet would come back to earth every seventy-two years. On the basis of this absolute "scientific fact", I spent many years of my life looking forward to this spectacular, once-in-a-lifetime event in 1986.

Came the year, I learned with disbelief (how could science be wrong?) that this time it would not pass very near the earth, would only be visible in the southern hemisphere, was not very bright this time, and so after all of those years of hope, I saw nothing. (Ah.......)

The comet may indeed return in another seventy two years' time, (well, forty two now,) but scientists no longer see this as a scientific fact, but a prediction, a good guess based on its previous behaviour. In over seventy years in deep space, anything could happen to Halley, including a cosmic traffic collision.

In the same way that the certainties of science seem to become less certain, so many of the past absolute certainties of faith are beginning to seem much less certain also. The Church's insistence on "the purity" of celibate clergy is a case in point, also the refusal to give women any public function in the Church These decisions are based on the grounds that this is what happened in the past, (not necessarily true) and presumably God can't cope with change.

But change has come. The twentieth century was a time of utter man-made devastation, which no one could have foretold a hundred years ago. There was an economic slump with millions out of work, the rise and fall of fascism and communism, two World Wars with millions displaced or slaughtered, great cities left in ruins, Europe and parts of Asia left in chaos, millions killed during the wars and in the aftermath, culminating in the use of two atom bombs dropped on Japan. Although they could make an atom bomb, knowledge of radiation sickness was very limited.

Since all of that, the Church's fine distinctions between venial and mortal sin no longer seems to have the same urgency or authority. Given what we know of how and why people behave in the way that they do, how on earth can we give totally rational, logical, final descriptions of God, and the universe? As the writers of the Scriptures knew, poetry, myth, symbolism give the only approximation to real answers.

When some Catholics say that the second Vatican Council was the beginning of the end, this can be easily understood, because that was the time when the Church obviously began to change, notably with the liturgy.

However, the cause of the Church's problems was not the second Vatican Council. The Church's problems had begun long, long before, with increasing centralisation and aspirations to total control. Vatican II made some problems plain and evident, but for many years, the Church has been slowly imploding under its own self-imposed inflexibility, the need to control everything, and its understandable ignorance of human psychology.

Most parish clergy realise that the absolute certainties of the old Penny Catechism do not even begin to touch many of the problems and difficulties of young people living in the twenty-first century and it seems that the catechism, is a symbol of much in the Church that needs rethinking.

Writing this chapter, I find myself comparing the modern Church to the image of a huge red star, a Gas Giant. These stars are very ancient; they have been giving out heat and light for billions of years and they have become so gigantic in size that their own planets are swallowed up. As they grow old their energy fails. With ever increasing size, the nuclear fires burn lower and the light becomes a dark red. The light and warmth they give becomes less and less.

Then the tired old sun finally implodes upon itself and collapses, but in so doing, it releases huge bursts of energy, seen as a brilliant light across thousands of light years of stars and galaxies – a nova. The light of the nova, the new light, suddenly bursts upon places unaware of the star's presence until then. The shining light of the old star is seen better than ever before, but as bright visible stardust, ready to make new creations. A Resurrection

The Church needs to give up the fantasy of total control, in order to realise that true faith comes from the heart, and not from the head. It was a great Catholic Frenchman and mystic, Pascal, who said that the heart has reasons that reason cannot understand - *La Coeur a ses raisons que la raison ne comprend pas.* (Pascal's Pensees)

The Church needs to care for real men and women and their real needs, physical, spiritual and psychological. It means letting people make up their own minds about their sexual lives with the absolute proviso that no harm is done to anyone, and recognising that people are often immature,, rather than sinful. (Difficult, because we humans are capable of constant self-delusion).

If the Church can direct its efforts to these things, instead of abstract, obsolete philosophy, grandiose organisation and discussions about refined points of doctrine and practice, maybe like the nova, a new spiritual miracle of resurrection can happen.

Chapter Thirteen

Ritual And Tradition

The Catholic Church is powerfully supported by the two pillars of Ritual and Tradition. Celebrating tradition is a universal human phenomenon; it is a vibrant aspect of humanity. All human institutions have their traditions and rituals

Psychologically, traditions give us strength; they make us feel that we belong to something much bigger than ourselves. We talk about "a great and proud tradition", we create traditions. In times of difficulty we tell ourselves stories about the past and we go on remembering and re-enacting them to give us the psychological strength and courage to survive.

Deep-seated traditions rarely go away, but they often change. The central Catholic tradition, the rite of the Mass, was founded on the back of the already ancient Jewish tradition of Passover, celebrated with a ritual meal. Far beyond this, originally it was probably a ritual to greet the spring.

HUMAN NEED FOR RITUAL

Because ritual and tradition are so important to us, there is, for instance, a deep human need to mark the departure of the dead, with more dignity than simply throwing the body into a hole or on to a fire without ceremony. When bodies are actually thrown into a hole, or onto a fire without ceremony, we feel anger at the betrayal of our common humanity.

Some years ago, I attended three Catholic funerals in two days. Well, almost. The third funeral was on television, and it was the broadcast funeral of Cardinal Archbishop Basil Hume, a much-loved and respected man. This was a very grand affair in Westminster Cathedral attended by monks, nuns, bishops, hundreds of priests, one or two cardinals, the Prime Minister, the Leader of the Opposition, representatives of the Pope and the English Royal family. There was a reverent hushed commentary from an experienced television commentator.

Sadly, I had attended two funerals of friends and colleagues, beforehand, one on the previous afternoon, and the other early in the morning before Cardinal Hume's funeral. The one thing that struck me, apart from the magnificence of the cardinal's funeral, was how similar they were. Give or take a few extra cardinals and bishops and some very grand music, the ritual was exactly the same for all three. I found myself thinking that when my turn came, my body would undergo exactly the same ritual, and this seemed enormously comforting, although because of the current shortage of priests, it may not....)

Rituals *are* very comforting. This is why we do them. Many believers, especially Catholics, seek to deepen their spirituality through ritual. For Catholics, the Mass, the Eucharist, is the great central ritual of all. We believe that the Mass unites us to God. Such traditions are spiritually and psychologically powerful, they centre us in the midst of a group, a nation, a religion. They give us spiritual strength in the midst of crisis; they also make us feel that we belong,

Then there are the popular traditions such as Bonfire Night or giving Easter Eggs, not to mention all the crazy preparations for Christmas. These are rituals with ancient origins, which emphatically mark the passing of the seasons, the passing of dark winter, and hope for spring. For Christians, Christmas and Easter mark the light of Christ coming into a dark world.

There used to be an old joke about "four wheeler Christians", who go to Church in a baby buggy for the Christening, a limousine for the wedding, and a hearse for the funeral. This does indicate clearly that everyone experiences an enormous need for ceremony and ritual to mark the great occasions of birth, life and death.

Those who no longer believe in Christianity, or other faiths, do not simply give up the rituals and traditions, instead, they devise new ones. There are many atheists who regret the loss of church going with its strong sense of community. Some have actually begun holding "Sunday Assemblies", where people who do not believe in God nevertheless meet to listen to music and readings, to sing together and enjoy silence, as well as enjoying the shared sense of community and welcome, and I believe that these are very popular.

We use ritual for celebration and for times of grief. The very earliest human beings, thousands of years ago buried their dead with ritual and ceremony and left gifts in the grave, including flowers. Ritual and tradition have a very long and ancient history, thousands of years old, much older than Christianity or any religion we know. It is deep in our bones. If any church or institution springs up fresh and new today, without being shackled to the old, it is a racing certainty that within two years it will have a whole raft of new traditions and rituals. Atheistic governments also have panoply of parades and public celebrations

Because of their enormous psychological power over human beings, traditions are a two-edged sword, for good or evil. Because of quarrels about tradition and ritual, families have been split apart, churches have been ripped into splinter groups, and countries have gone to war.

Even rituals which are intended to bring people closer together, can be used as a means of ripping them apart, if insisted on in a closed spirit of anger and bitterness. This is shown clearly in the bitter, yet hilarious description of Christmas dinner, in *Portrait of the Artist as a Young Man,* by James Joyce.

The rituals of the Church are of central importance to Catholics, much more so than theology. Baptism, Communion, Confirmation, Marriage, ordination, the anointing of the sick and the Mass, these are the rituals that bind us together, and make us who we are. The Mass is the greatest ritual of all. Priests have risked torture and death, and given their lives, in order to be able to say Mass, and ordinary Catholics have risked their lives in order to attend Mass and receive communion. This is why it is tragic that the current shortage of priests means fewer and fewer celebrations of Mass.

What then did Freud think of rituals? He thought that they were the marks of deep unconscious anxiety. He believed that everyone, especially neurotic people, that is, emotionally damaged people, unconsciously, carried out rituals in order to calm themselves down. In this way, men and women try to relieve their anxiety, but, if they are really ill, they invariably fail and are impelled to carry out the ritual over and over again.

The rituals I have just written about, mostly created consciously and publicly for some big event, have the effect of uniting the observers in shared emotion or feelings. In rituals connected with birth, marriage or death, or the seasons of the year, there is bound to be an enormous amount of anxiety.

There are other, more personal rituals which we all recognise, such as the rituals which we carry out to calm ourselves before going to bed - having a nightcap, tidying the living room, locking the door, putting out the lights, setting the alarm clock, brushing our teeth, maybe even saying our prayers. These rituals are a message to ourselves that we are about to close down for the night.

COMPULSIVE RITUALS

There are also the really serious unconscious acts called compulsive rituals, which Freud noticed when he was working with his patients. These consist of constantly repeated actions such as hand washing, or compulsive cleaning, which the sufferer seems totally unable to stop or prevent. This is where Freud derived his ideas about anxiety.

A well-known example of this was Dr. Johnson, the writer of the first English Dictionary, who had many strange tics or habits. Living in eighteenth century London, he was incapable of walking along a street without compulsively touching every street post he passed, and this had the result of making him walk strangely from side to side. This must have been the result of some deep childhood anxiety or fear.

After the First World War it was realised that as the result of the hideous slaughter in the most appalling conditions, many of the men and officers developed tics, or obsessive behaviour, or even an inability to see or speak, which had entirely mental and emotional causes and not physical. Further studies along this line have led modern therapists to label this sort of problem as Obsessive Compulsive Disorder. Someone with this disorder finds herself repeatedly carrying out certain actions, and is unable to control the urges of the unconscious mind.

A brilliant example of an unconscious ritual is Shakespeare's Lady Macbeth. Her husband, Macbeth, had murdered King Duncan, who was a relative of his. Moving the knives at the scene of the crime, her hands, like her husband's, had been covered in blood.

At the time she dismissed this as trivial, asserting that, "a little water clears us of this deed", but although she has consciously tried to suppress her guilt, unconsciously she is unable to do so. Night after night, she compulsively stalks the castle corridors in her sleep, ritually wringing her hands as if to wash them of blood and guilt

"Out, out damned spot. Who would have thought that the old man had so much blood in him?" she cries in her sleepwalking despair.

This is a first class example of what Freud called "the return of the repressed". Although consciously cold and emotionless at the time of the murder, she had been severely traumatised. Unconsciously she was trying to rid herself of the pain of that trauma by repeating the scene in her sleep and trying to overcome it.

I myself, as a young girl, had a strange ritual when I was on the bus going to school. The bus travelled the length of one very long street, which had only terrace houses, no shops, all exactly the same, two doors, two windows, on and on without a break. I had developed a nervous habit of trying to tap with my feet the exact pattern of doors and windows all along the street. Of course, as the bus speeded up, this became impossible, and I was obliged to give up.

The strange thing was that although I knew that it was impossible to do, I nevertheless felt a strong compulsion to try to do this every morning. It was, of course, a deep anxiety about going to school, because I did not feel the slightest need to do this when coming back in the afternoon.

The British army is full of ritual, what is called "bull" - parades, saluting, wearing smart uniforms and highly polished boots and badges. The aim of these rituals, especially drill, is specifically to reduce anxiety in soldiers who deal daily with violence and death. Soldiers risk their lives on a daily basis, but ritual behaviour decreases their anxiety. There is an even greater problem, which is that they will have to kill others, and the ritual of intensive drill is intended to remove both fear and guilt.

Sparkling cleanliness and brilliantly shining badges disguise the dirt and blood of war. Fear of the Sergeant Major becomes greater than fear of the enemy, with the hope of making the soldier more efficient. However, excessive, inflexible "bull" may make soldiers less efficient in certain circumstances, such as jungle warfare.

A more deeply buried example of unconscious ritual is in Mrs. Gaskell's beautiful novel *Cranford*. There have been robberies in the neighbourhood of Cranford, and the elderly lady, Miss Matty, is so nervous of someone breaking into the house, that she has a nightly ritual of rolling a ball under her bed, to make sure that there is no man hiding there.

This nightly ritual of rolling the ball under the bed is obviously to calm Miss Matty's anxiety. However, it fails, because she feels compelled to do this every time she goes to bed, even though the doors are locked and there are at least two other people in the house. This is because her anxiety is not really about burglars at all, but something quite different.

As a tender-hearted young woman, Miss Matty's hopes of marriage were dashed by her controlling father and possibly her sister's jealousy. Although after many years, she is consciously reconciled to her lot as an old maid under her sister's control, deep in her heart, Miss Matty had never really given up hope of seeing her suitor again. I am sure Freud would have said that for Miss Matty, unconsciously, the non-existent man under her bed symbolised her lost lover.

CATHOLIC RITUAL

For Catholics, the ritual of the Mass is the ceremony in which we feel that we contact the divine and are joined together as one - maybe we too are seeking a lost lover. We believe we are re-enacting the Last Supper, sharing in the wealth of life and grace of Jesus. Receiving Communion, we believe, is a way in which we share powerfully in the love of God and the Catholic Family. Baptisms often take place during Mass, Catholic weddings have a Nuptial Mass as part of the ceremony, and there is a Requiem Mass for funerals – or at least there was, until the shortage of priests became so acute.

Some of the men who have power and influence in the Church are obviously pathologically controlling; they want things to be done precisely in the way they think proper, in exact precise accordance with the exact ancient rules of the ritual. Their purpose in doing this can only be to calm their own unconscious fears and anxiety.

Since the Church Council of Vatican II, there have been upheavals in the main ritual of the Church. The most obvious modern change has been the change from the universal use of Latin as the language of the Mass, in favour of the vernacular, the local language, in whichever country the Mass is said.

Most Catholics accepted this with little fuss, and great joy and the movement was accompanied by changes in music and different patterns of behaviour. It has been cheerfully accepted and welcomed by Mass go-ers everywhere. However, a comparatively small number of people, very vocal, and some of them extremely influential, were very upset by this, and continue to be so. They seek to impose their ideas on everyone else as the "correct" way to do things.

Gradually, and especially under the guidance of the Emeritus Pope Benedict, it became more possible to celebrate the old "Tridentine" Mass in Latin on a regular basis. This seems reasonable, as it was the only form of Mass for well over a thousand years, but there is a movement in the Church, which regards the Latin Mass, with plainsong as the only "proper" Mass, and is suspicious, sometimes contemptuous even, of everybody who wants the Mass in the vernacular, or maybe with different music.

A TWO EDGED SWORD

Love of one another is the most central belief in the Church, but it can be ignored in bitter anger about the nature of tradition and ritual, especially if someone depends on exact ritual for their own personal, mental balance. In France, such was the anger (and anxiety) of Archbishop Lefebre that he split off from the Church and now leads his own schismatic group, which has become in effect, a separate church since he consecrated his own bishops.

These groups have a deep devotion to the Latin Mass. It is, I think, a desire to reach a true spirituality. sI believe that the changes of Vatican II have been unbearably terrifying for some traditionalists. These are people with a deep need for ritual to allay their anxieties about life, possibly as a result of an anxious childhood, trauma, abandonment or separation, such as being sent to a boarding school (or seminary) at a very early age,

Tradition can be a wonderful thing, but, I repeat, it is a two edged sword. When it leads to rigidity, anger, rage and harsh judgements of others, it becomes a stumbling block. There is a problem if the tradition is used as an excuse for unkindness, abuse of power, contempt or the personal emotional need for total control of others.

Control of others is also a powerful way of coping with deep personal anxiety, in the same way that those who insist on compulsory celibacy for clergy indicate a deep unconscious anxiety about sex.

There is no reason why people should not have a devotion to the Latin Mass, though superficial matters of rites and clothing seem to be attractive to some young priests who are trying to go back to the old ways. This is probably because English bishops have deliberately chosen very conservative "safe pair of hands" clergy to be responsible for priestly formation. For instance, wearing the tasselled black cap called a "biretta" seems to some to be a mark of holiness. This shows intense anxiety, which is relieved by "getting it right", by having the proper ritual in its exact form. If the ritual is not correctly performed, it is unconsciously believed that something terrible will happen.

Intense anxiety about the forms and details of ritual shows an overwhelming desire to "be good", to please one's inner "parents". This is far from mature religion or spirituality, but shows a very primitive and even a childish idea of God, usually caused by deep fear in childhood. There are probably very good deep-seated, personal reasons for some of these people to be intensely anxious.

A real problem occurs when the precision of the ritual causes even greater worry than the anxiety it is supposed to be calming. Sometimes, people can become fixated on traditional ritualistic details, in order to forget the reality of what is happening in their own daily lives.

This was clearly seen in the First World War. This was a totally different war to any that had taken place previously. The British Army had been trained for over a hundred years to stay together in blocks and then fire together, without moving from their positions. Then, on the order, they fixed bayonets and charged the enemy. The trouble was that the English soldiers with the fixed bayonets were now charging, not against other soldiers with swords and bayonets, but against men with machine guns who mowed them down by the thousand.

Given their inability to change tactics, in the face of daily losses of hundreds of thousands of men, some Generals went into denial, ignored the losses, and concentrated on spit and polish, shining badges, looking smart on Parade, and saluting any officer who happened to be passing.

> *"Good morning; good morning," the General said......*
> *...He's a cheery old cove grunted Harry to Jack,*
> *As they slogged up to Arras with rifle and pack,*
> *But he did for them both by his plan of attack.*
> *Siegfried Sassoon*

Similar anxiety is shown in the English TV comedy series, "Dad's Army" about the Second World War. A fictional Home Guard officer, the inadequate Captain Mainwaring, faced with the impossible task of getting a bunch of eccentric geriatrics to fight the Nazis when they come, takes refuge in rituals, spit and polish, and pomposity.

DENIAL

I fear that some leaders of the Church have been in a similar position, using old traditions to cope with totally new situations. Trying to restore ancient rituals, such as the use of Latin, has been used to try to control a Church where thousands of young (and middle aged) people are simply leaving in droves (many of them because of the teaching on birth control).

Large rallies of young people to meet the Pope in Catholic countries simply disguise the reality. There are, in Europe, America and Australia, fewer and fewer priests, most of them very old, and in many cases past retirement, but nevertheless hanging on. Churches are closed, parishes are merged, which in turn are merged with other merged parishes, and the Western Catholic Church appears to be going down the plughole.

In many parts of the world, including Europe, it is no longer always possible to have a Requiem Mass for the dead because of priestly shortages and funerals are carried out by trained members of the laity. For many Catholics this is the last straw. We are at ease about the laity, but we find it hard that there should be no Mass.

For some members of the Vatican Curia, the reaction to this is the same as for the Generals of World War I.

- First Denial. Change nothing, tell people to pray for vocations. Insist that if we are really holy Catholics, the young priests will come pouring in and all will be as it was before. Ignore the losses, and insist that if we keep on keeping on, the day will be saved. Cling to the ideal of clerical celibacy, even though most Catholics would like to bring back priests who left the priesthood in order to get married. The shortage of clergy is already way past crisis point.
- Second, concentrate on the detail of ritual. Special rites, special forms, old ways of celebrating Mass can be brought back. Think about the vestments, the look of the thing. A number of customs have been recently revived which earlier Popes had let go.
- Third, insist on superficial unity. To the intense annoyance of most English speaking Bishops, the Vatican has insisted that all English-speaking Catholics, all over the world, use one new translation of the Latin Mass, and one only. This includes the USA, Canada, The British Isles, Australia, New Zealand and parts of Africa and Asia.

The fact that all of these people speak completely different forms of English, (even New Zealand English is different from Australian English) with different grammar and vocabulary, and words used in a different sense, is totally overlooked by the Vatican Curia, who seem to think that dissent is trivial, a "let them eat cake" mentality.

The protests of local bishops are completely ignored and over-ridden. Also, very many last minute changes were made in Rome, by "traditionalists" who seem to have little, if any, literary or linguistic ability. The resulting so called "English" is hideous beyond belief.

It has been impossible to complain about this, because the Vatican clerical civil service, the Curia, ignores the bishops. What has emerged is a version of the Mass that satisfies few English speakers, annoys the majority and sounds foreign to many people. This is seen as less important than the superficial unity acquired. The result is a great deal of sadness and confusion, about the great ritual of the Mass, which is of central importance to all Catholics.

So ritual, a comforting and deeply meaningful means of celebrating one's Catholicism, is under attack by groups of Catholics who apparently are suffering from an obsessive compulsion, based on their own private pathology. Some of these have deeply anxious personalities and spend a lot of time worrying about the nature of the ceremonies and the translation of the text used. Their new translation is spreading anxiety among those Catholics who were quite happy with the use of their local language. Anxiety spreads anxiety.

A very good instance of this occurred recently in my locality. A parish priest who was ordained after Vatican II, so has never said a Latin Mass, felt that those who do miss it, should be listened to, and he agreed to allow the old Latin Mass regularly in his church. He himself would not say the Mass, but the group involved would arrange for a visiting priest. Imagine the parish priest's horror when, after the first Latin Mass, he received a bitter and vicious letter from a member of the visiting congregation, accusing him of not doing things properly in his church and which sneeringly concluded that nothing more could be expected of a priest like him.

The parish priest reacted angrily, and the letter writer was forced by his group to apologise profusely. Here is it obvious that saying the Mass in Latin, according to the preferred version, did nothing to decrease the letter writer's fear and anxiety, or increase his Christian charity. Instead of experiencing joy, his fears and anxieties actually increased, and were expressed in bitterness. His intense fear was that even now, when it seemed right, the precise rituals were not being followed exactly and in the correct spirit. His anxiety made him almost hysterical with rage.

This of course, is magical thinking and according to Freud, neurotic – emotionally ill. Magical thinking insists that if the ritual is not correctly followed to the letter, terrible results will follow. It is like small children avoiding the cracks in the pavement in case the bears come and get them.

The Church, all churches, have many rituals, some more elaborate than others. They are a part of being alive, a part of celebrating being Christian. Much of the infighting about the form it takes is about deep personal anxiety, not about the nature of Christianity. St. Paul himself, two thousand years ago had problems – some of the early Christians were deeply anxious and outraged by the way in which others lived and celebrated their Christianity. There were huge arguments about the need for converts to be circumcised, or forbidding them to eat meat which had been offered to idols (anxiety again). St. Paul said simply that love, charity, should be the guiding principle.

Jesus put it very simply, "Judge not, lest you be judged". According to St. John, he also said that "True worshippers will worship in spirit and in truth" which sounds very anxiety free.

The leading authorities in the Curia are not likely to lose their anxiety, and maybe some of them need to be replaced. Ordinary lay Catholics are not some sort of mentally deficient underclass to be ordered around, but really committed men and women who are sensitive to their own spiritual needs, and have enormous amounts of insight to contribute.

Chapter Fourteen

Without Love, Children Die.

In the middle ages, Frederick II, King of Sicily and Holy Roman Emperor, known as "The Wonder of the World", made the first known experiment about children needing love. This experiment was made, about eight hundred years ago, with live children.

In the first half of the thirteenth century, some enlightened person had told the king that children could not even live without love; they could not survive. Frederick, although cruel, was of an enquiring mind and decided to set up an experiment. He took two newborn baby boys from somewhere and had them brought up in a large room in a castle.

The king ordered that the babies were to be given every encouragement to live, except love. They had food, warmth and clothing; in many ways they had luxury. At first they had "wet nurses" to breast feed them. The guards were instructed that they themselves were not to talk to the children or show them kindness, and they were to make sure that the women who cared for them did not speak to them, smile at them or play with them. They were to care for the physical needs of the babies and then go. Guards and nurses probably changed fairly frequently.

At first, the babies seemed to thrive physically, and they had one another for company, and probably developed some sort of language of their own but they both died in early childhood. After a few years one died first, and the other, left totally alone and friendless, deprived of his only companion, died a few months later. You could say that Frederick's cruel experiment was successful; he had proved that children could not survive without love and affection. They were fed and clothed, but this was not enough. As a priest I once knew used to say, "The operation was successful, but the patient died". It was a hideously cruel experiment, but it made the truth clear.

THE "GOOD ENOUGH" MOTHER

Early in the twentieth century, scientists made a similar experiment, but this time with baby chimpanzees. Female baby chimpanzees were taken from their mothers and kept in separate cages. In order to give them some sort of artificial normality, each cage was equipped with two imitation mothers made of wood and wire.

The models were made roughly in the shape of a mother chimpanzee, with a very crude head on top. One of the models was simply wood and wire, but was fitted with a container with a nipple and plenty of milk, so that the baby chimp could have food whenever it wanted. The other model was also of wood and wire, without the milk, but covered with towelling, so that it felt soft and comfortable.

Most of the time, the baby would cling to the soft towelling "mother" and from time to time would clamber across to the wire mother for food, and then go back to clinging to the towelling. But there was no cuddling, holding, chattering, teaching, grooming, not even a clout on the ear, which would have been attention of a sort.

These baby chimps were introduced to other animals when they were old enough to feed themselves, and eventually mated and had babies of their own. They were never able to mix with the others successfully, were bullied and ill-treated and had none of the natural liveliness of young animals. When they mated and had babies, they had no idea at all of how to be mothers. They ignored their offspring and neglected them, did not care for them or groom them, because they had no idea how to.

This is what happens to humans who have lacked a proper carer.

D.W. Winnicott, a famous doctor and therapist, who worked with children, invented the term "a good enough mother" to describe the sort of parent children need, to become reasonably capable and responsible adults.

Everyone needs a "good enough mother". Not an ideal mother, or a saint, but a good enough mother. The problem is not to *make* people "behave more responsibly" but to treat everyone, especially children, with love and respect, so that they then know in their bones, because they have experienced it, that everyone deserves love and care.

I am not talking about sentimentality, but affection, compassion, respect and generosity, the sort of love that is contemptuous of no-one, and wishes evil to no-one. In the words of St. Paul to the Corinthians, "love is always patient and kind; it is never jealous; love is never boastful or conceited; it is never rude or selfish; it does not take offence, and is not resentful. Love takes no pleasure in other people's sins; but delights in the truth. It is always ready to excuse, to trust, to hope, to endure whatever comes." Of course, most human beings, let alone most mothers, would fail at least some of these hurdles.

Counsellors and therapists often experience powerful feelings of despair, anger, fear, jealousy, resentfulness etc., unconnected with their own lives, while they are working with a client. They are in fact experiencing their clients' feelings. This is called "transference", and gives an enormous insight into the emotional life of the clients, what is really worrying them, and what they may be unable to say in words.

We know only too well that within us we are often jealous and conceited, often selfish, and often take offence, especially if we are sensitive souls. We are often resentful, often want to punish wrongdoing harshly, and do not always delight in the truth. Very often these feelings are unconscious so that we sabotage our own efforts. If however, we can understand that we are like this, and understand the pathological origins of many of these feelings in ourselves, and if we are lucky enough to experience nurturing care, we may be able to overcome them.

CHILD KILLERS

When we have the instances of children behaving in savage ways, such as those of child murderers who kill other little children, this is not because they are "born evil" but made so, by adults who treated them contemptuously, cruelly and harshly, and totally ignored their emotional needs. The notorious case of Mary Bell, the little girl who strangled a smaller boy has been intensively investigated by Gitta Sereny, who has exposed the terrible childhood which Mary experienced, in her book, *Cries Unheard, The Story of Mary Bell*.

Mary's prostitute mother, who herself was seriously disturbed, hated her from birth. Mary, the little girl who was described as "a monster" by the privileged, white, male judge, came from a background of neglect, hatred and sadistic sexual abuse during which she would be half strangled for perverse sexual satisfaction, by one of her mother's clients. As a result she strangled a little boy. Psychologically, this is called "repetitive compulsion". The abused child feels compelled to repeat over and over again what has been done to them. Being only a child, Mary could not know when to stop.

In this sort of context, how can we possibly talk of this little girl committing sin, which is an offence against God, which needs to be punished? An offence against God it may be, it was also an offence against Mary.

It was a serious offence for the judge to call her "a monster". Newspaper editors also like to use this sort of language. The child had already endured suffering beyond bearing, and this is what made her what she was. Nor is she the only one. *Adults who abuse children sexually, including priests, were almost invariably abused themselves as children.* This is not new, this sort of evil has been going on for thousands of years, and is a terrible life-destroying disease, an emotional cancer, not an intellectual misunderstanding, or a lack of will power.

What we call "virtue" is the result of kindness and good treatment, if not in the beginning of life, then later. It cannot be taught in an abstract way, not with severity or harshness, or law, or boot camps, prisons or anything else, it can only be developed if the seeds of love and respect have been there from the beginning. If the child never finds love, you end up with someone who is very sick indeed. On the other hand, if someone, somewhere, loves you, an aunt, a grandmother, or a good friend, things may change.

Without love, and faced by hideous abuse of one sort or another, the child may grow up be criminally insane, without any sense of remorse, a psychopath. This is why some adopted children have huge difficulties, because they are often passed from one adult to another during the early stages of life, and constantly lose the people they become attached to. A constant change of "carers" is one of the worst things that can happen to a child, because it learns that love will always be snatched away. Unconsciously, the child learns that in order to avoid pain and loss, it is better not to love anyone.

REHABILITATION

There were some documentary films that were very popular a few years ago. The idea was to take some young thugs who thought they were tough, but who had been in a lot of trouble with the police. These lads were taken to some remote place – a mountainous area, a ship, or an island maybe. Here they were put through rigorous army exercises, extremely hard work, tramping, hiking, and mountaineering while carrying heavy loads, usually under the tuition of some very hard-bitten and experienced sergeant from the army.

Very often this had an extraordinary effect; gradually this bunch of lazy, selfish individualists became a team. Gradually they learned to help one another; gradually they learned respect for one another and they became friends. They were given interviews later, and asked what had happened to them and why. With difficulty they would explain that the respect they had learned during this experiment had changed their lives. They had learned to respect others, and they had learned to respect themselves, they felt of value to society and were they could be responsible members of society.

Something similar was done more recently, in a TV programme with men who had problems and were sent to live in a monastery for a while, and were subject to the same sort of discipline as the monks, though somewhat moderated. Similar results came. After a great deal of soul searching, time in chapel and gardening, they found great changes in their lives and became more balanced members of society.

There you are, says the saloon bar philosopher. Proves it. All they needed was a bit of discipline, a bit of boot camp and their lives are changed, they became responsible and useful members of society. Discipline is what matters. Or is it?

The same experiment was undertaken in a community of enclosed nuns, and although the nuns did their best the results were somewhat mixed, and there were some obvious failures. Was this because women were less good at discipline than men?

Well no. I do know through a friend who knew some of the nuns in question, that they were rather more naïve than the monks. The monks insisted on vetting the men who were sent to them, and did not accept people who were mentally ill. This meant that all of the men in their programme were genuine searchers for some sort of healing spirituality.

The nuns, were, as I said, either more naïve, or more inclusive. They did not make any such stipulation, and the producers of the programme wanted a bit of excitement and provocation. Some of the women who were sent along were very seriously disturbed, and could not really escape from their own deep problems sufficiently to co-operate with the spiritual discipline and psychological help that was offered to them.

Discipline was not the only thing at work here. There were a great many other factors at work. To begin with these people were taken out of their familiar surroundings, but not, as in prison, for years of dreary existence and punishment.

In the army experiment, the new surroundings were mostly out of doors. The men lived at very close quarters in fairly tough conditions. They were also given a great deal of very expensive equipment and clothing. They knew, of course, that they were being televised. They were given tasks, targets, something to aim for. The hope was that some great change would come about in their lives. Every day they were set some new exciting challenge, presented as something they could achieve, however unlikely that had seemed when they first began the course. They were constantly encouraged to take pride in their courage, ability, and their smartness.

Similarly in the religious community experiment, they were taken out of their usual surroundings, not to a prison, where they would be surrounded by lots of other disturbed characters, but a well established convent or monastery, well organised, clean and aesthetically pleasing. Pictures, candles, soothing ritual, prayer and well designed buildings were all part of a situation which must have given them a sense of something more beautiful and meaningful than the hassle of their every day lives. Gardening formed a large part of their activities in beautiful grounds. They had clean, comfortable, if plain living quarters, and regular well-served meals.

The main figure in all of these programmes was the mentor. For the soldiers it was the hard-bitten sergeant, but he was obviously well chosen. Not only was he tough and disciplined, but here was a man you felt instinctively that you could trust your life to. So great was the fantasy, that even I, a seventy year old woman, felt that with someone like that in charge, I too could run up mountains carrying impossible loads. (As Terry Pratchet has observed, whole economies have been built on the carrying power of little old ladies dressed in black.)

You felt that beneath this steely exterior was a man who cared and who wanted these men to succeed. He would do anything to ensure that they did succeed, and his pride when they did succeed was enormous and made evident. He told them repeatedly that they had worth, that they were valuable, and eventually would be men he could be proud of, and who could be admired. Say it quietly, but he loved them.

This is one aspect of the army that is often overlooked, but the army's role as a caring mother is a matter of fact. Many men who leave the army are unable to cope with civilian life. Soldiers are cared for, cherished, punished, forgiven, sent into impossible situations, given praise and medals, and enormous pride in themselves. It is not by chance that one of the popular World War I marching songs was;

> *"Kiss me good night Sergeant Major,*
> *Sergeant Major be a mother to me."*

The same thing happened in the monastery and convent situations. Each candidate, and all were volunteers remember, were given some sort of special mentor, who talked to them, listened to them and their problems, worked with them and attended the chapel with them.

In other words, these people were given not only a disciplined, orderly situation but also an enormous amount of care and attention – more than they had ever experienced in their lives before, on a daily basis. I speak here of only the care and attention we could see. There were presumably many other instances. Preparations for the programme, interviews, choices being made as to whether these people were suitable for the experience, though as I have said, I believe that the nuns were short-changed on this one.

There were camera crews, production teams, and above all perhaps, the knowledge that this would be seen by thousands, maybe millions of people (it was prime time TV) all rooting for them to succeed.

In short, these people were surrounded by an enormous amount of positive attention, interest and care. Is it surprising then that they emerged from the experience quite changed and very Responsible?

The dark side of this is that soldiers who work and live heroically with their mates in the army, are often unable to cope with civilian life, because they cannot cope without the constant care and supervision and especially the companionship of their mates.

In these cases the "good enough mother" is a mother who brutally abandons her children. For creating responsibility for life, love is more important than discipline. If discipline is infused by love, it may produce remarkable results. Without love, harsh discipline brutalises and is simply another fuel for anger and resentment.

THE NEED TO CONNECT

Babies are born, not with original sin, but with a desperate need to belong, to connect, to relate, to love. If this is not satisfied during the early months of childhood, the loss is rarely, if ever, made up. This is now proved beyond dispute by the study of neuroscience.

In Sue Gerhardt's very readable book on neuroscience, *Why Love Matters,* she explains, clearly and in detail, how sadness and grief in early childhood creates actual physical changes in the brain. These changes can last a lifetime, unless the child receives enormous help. When the child experiences loss or rejection, the brain is flooded with cortisol, a chemical which is associated with depression.

One of the major stresses which a child can experience is loss of the mother. Loss of several carers, or "mothers" is a thousand times worse. With each loss, the chemical cortisol, either reflecting or causing depression, floods the brain and eventually excess cortisol becomes the normal situation. A sense of loss becomes permanent.

Too much cortisol in the brain can leave the child or adult open to all sorts of infection or mental illness, a loss of energy and the power to act and do things. If the suffering is continued, the cortisol does not go away, and in the face of repeated difficulties and frustrations, the cortisol keeps returning. This leads to intense depression, emotional paralysis and often to physical illness. This is why an elderly man or woman may die of cancer, shortly after a much loved partner dies.

For many people who are constantly ill, throughout their lives, this probably began in babyhood, and although some scientists may deny it, is often more to do with feelings than genes but this does not mean that the illness is imagined, or can easily be got rid of.

On the other hand, joy, the repeated smile and loving laughter on the mother's face, or the experience of good feeding, causes chemicals such as dopamine (which is used to help people with Parkinson's disease) or serotonin to flood the brain, and this brings peace and happiness. If, of course, the mother is always talking on her mobile phone or watching TV when feeding the child, and ignoring the baby, dopamine lessens and cortisol increases.

For this reason, the baby buggy in which the baby is facing forward, and cannot see its mother's face, but only the wheels of lorries, or the oncoming crowds, is disastrous from a child development point of view.

The brain systems that enable us to love or to hate, to have courage or paralysing terror, are all developed and settled within the first two years of life. Many things can happen after that which may be traumatic, but the basic psychology of the child is settled. This is why some people can endure, and more easily recover from trauma by which others are destroyed. This is why some men could survive the horrors of war in the trenches during the First World War, and others were mentally destroyed with what was called "shell shock". This is why some people are more able to face the stresses and strains of life than others, without too much difficulty. Even if sufferings in later life are horrendous, those who have experienced much love in the first few years of life, have a distinct advantage for survival.

Love, as St. Paul said, means compassion, generosity, unselfishness and care for others. It is not a sentimental, religious add-on, bolted onto life, which the tough man or woman can do without. Love, as Jesus well knew and taught unceasingly, is essential to life, it makes life possible. Without love of any sort, or the memory of love, however inadequate, we just lie down and die. Love increases health and the ability to cope with life's hardships, it increases real joy; it makes us creative instead of destructive and enables us to relate more easily to others and respond generously to their needs. Bad behaviour in later years is not merely a matter of will, but of severe emotional deprivation in early life.

This is why Freud believed that the good relationship with the analyst was a major reason for the success of "the talking cure." This is why kind and friendly priests get better results than judgmental ones. When Jesus spoke of bringing love to the world and said that he came to bring Life, and bring it more abundantly, this is not just "religion", for he was speaking the literal truth.

St. Paul in the thirteenth chapter of his Letter to the Corinthians, voiced the creed of the early church;

"If I have all the eloquence of men or of angels, but speak without love, I am simply a gong booming or a cymbal clashing. If I have the gift of prophecy, understanding all the mysteries there are, and knowing everything, and if I have faith in all its fullness, to move mountains, but without love, then I am nothing at all. If I give away all that I possess, piece by piece, and if I even let them take my body to burn it, but am without love, it will do me no good whatever.

Love is always patient and kind; it is never rude or selfish, it dos not take offence, and is not resentful. Love takes no pleasure in other people's sins, but delights in the truth, it is always ready to excuse, to trust to hope..."

Chapter Fifteen

Dreams And Visions

Dreams Are The Royal High Road To The Unconscious.

Freud

Your sons and daughters shall prophesy, your old men shall dream dreams, and your young men shall see visions.

Prophet Joel

I am writing this shortly after Christmas, and there has been a lot of talk in Church about dreams. These dreams are, of course the dreams in the Christmas stories. Normally Catholics don't seem to place too much confidence in dreams – good solid instruction in the faith is usually seen as much more important. Yet the stories at the very beginning of the gospel are full of them.

In the New Testament, we read that Mary's husband, Joseph, who is mostly ignored by the Church, had several dreams. We are told that when Mary was found to be pregnant before marriage, Joseph, being a just man had decided to "put Mary away" privately, but he had a dream in which an angel told him to marry her.

Later, after Jesus was born, when Herod was killing boy children, in order to protect his throne, Joseph had another dream in which an angel told him to take Mary and Jesus to Egypt. There are other stories of angels taking messages, but the rest of the gospel stories, about Jesus' life, do not really mention this much except when, shortly before the crucifixion, Pilate's wife told her husband that she had had a warning in a dream, to tell him not to have anything to do with "this just man".

The Old Testament too has many references to dreams, including the famous dreams of Joseph, which Lloyd Weber was to use so brilliantly in his musical, *Joseph and the Technicolour Dreamcoat.* Weber uses the dreams of Joseph as a basis of a whole life of aspiration.

There is a dream of St. Peter, in the *Acts of the Apostles.* Paul, who had lived outside Israel, was anxious that Christianity should be preached to everyone in the whole world. Peter, a more stay-at-home man, who may never have left the shores of Galilee until he met Jesus, was doubtful, hesitated, and had no idea what to do.

In his dream, or vision, Peter was shown an image of a sheet, let down from heaven, containing all sorts of "animals, reptiles and birds" which were forbidden as food by the strict laws of the Jews. In his dream, Peter was told to kill some of these and eat them. For Jews, these were banned as food altogether. They were "unclean", not fit for human consumption. Even those animals and birds, which it was quite all right to eat, had to be killed in a kosher manner, draining the blood, which takes time.

Dreaming Peter, looking at the cloth full of "unclean" animals, and ordered to kill and eat some of them, was revolted, felt ill at the thought, and as an observant Jew protested. This was against his culture and religion. In his dream, he protested to the Voice that he had never eaten anything unclean, but was told that he must not call *unclean* those things which God had called *clean.*

Peter eventually realised that this powerful dream was not about food, but about future Christians. All people are clean. All people are acceptable, and no one is to be rejected. This did not come about because of a long discussion between all interested parties, but was the result of a vision by someone who knew Jesus.

FREUD AND DREAMS

Freud wrote a book about the importance and origin of dreams, and firmly believed that this would be the one thing for which he would be remembered. He believed that *all dreams are messages*, but – and it is a big but - the message is not from an external God, or the Devil, or any other external agency, but from deep within the dreamer

For this reason, Freud would always listen attentively to his patients when they told him about their dreams. From the depth of the imaginative self, the state of the soul is represented by the images that haunt us in our sleep. He was convinced that anyone who wished to understand the working of his own soul should analyse his dreams, either alone, or with the help of a therapist or friend. Every day, he analysed his own dreams, and often those of his friends. He described the dream world grandly as "the royal highroad to the unconscious".

This way of working deepens the spiritual world of the dreamer. It gives us imaginative access to the depths of our own souls.

In the middle ages, Francis of Assisi went to see Pope Innocent III for permission to begin his order of wandering friars, poor friars with a dream of preaching the gospel, serving the poor, and of *being* poor without monasteries or money, and was rejected. It was a hard time for the Church, and the Pope was convinced that the Church was collapsing – maybe much as it seems now to many of us. There had been Crusades and Holy

Wars, but they only seemed to make matters worse. The Pope really didn't need this man dressed in tatty old clothes and claiming to be able to save the world through kindness and talking to animals.

That night, when Francis had gone, the Pope went to bed, anxious and troubled. When he finally fell asleep, he had a dream in which he was in a Church that was decrepit and falling down, and the roof was about to collapse. In his dream the poor man Francis, in his old clothes, came into this ruin of a Church. He looked round and stretched out his arms. Then, holding them up high, he held up the roof of the Church, which had been about to cave in.

When he woke, the Pope was deeply moved by this. He felt convinced that Francis, the poor man of peace and love, would hold up the collapsing Church where kings, wealth and armies could not. Was this a message from "out there" from God?

Far from being a message from "out there" this dream, according to Freud's methods, represented the deepest and most hidden wish and belief of the Pope. It also meant that although cold reason told him that Francis was a waste of space, his unconscious emotions were full of trust and confidence in this strange little man.

He did not dare think it, it seemed so outrageous, irrational and uncontrolled, and so he had a dream instead. Francis was called back to the Pope, and given permission to begin his order of poor brothers, who were to spread across Europe, work in towns and still exist today. They had a huge part to play in the development of the first universities of Europe. The present Pope has taken the name Francis.

At first, Freud believed that dreams were always the manifestation of deep desires, and without question, dreams of desire are very common. Prisoners starving in concentration camps dreamed of food, and ordinary prisoners in prisons dream often of sex, or maybe running freely along the beach and so on.

TRAUMATIC DREAMS

After the First World War, however, Freud heard of many dreams, which were certainly not dreams of desire, in which some terrible explosion, some terrible trauma was repeated over and over in the dream.

It was impossible to believe that the men who had these dreams wished for the repeat of some hideous traumatic event. So we now understand that people have anxiety or traumatic dreams. The dreamer goes over and over the same terrible material, hoping for a solution or healing. Many nightmares fall into this category, and are often the result of deep trauma in infancy. An old lady I once knew was sent to an orphanage for two years as a little girl, when her mother died. She was so young that she could not remember the experience, but for the rest of her life she was haunted by dreams of running down corridors, frantically looking for someone.

Because of Freud we now know that the only way to clear these horrible dreams is to be able to talk about them to someone we trust, over and over again, until they begin to lose their power.

Carl Jung, at one time a close colleague of Freud, felt that the dream is a message from the unconscious, not necessarily a desire, but a representation of what is going on in the dreamer's innermost self, and this does more often seem to fit the case of the traumatic dream.

So what is going on in the innermost self? Well practically anything, sorrow, anger, grief, inspiration, desire of all sorts, love, hatred, joy, frequently anxiety, because dreams are not about logical things, but about our feelings. Trying to understand our dreams can only deepen the knowledge of the riches within us.

Maybe there are Christians who would feel a sense of loss if they were told that the dreams in the Bible are not directly from God. We need to remember Jesus' saying that "the kingdom of God is within you," these "messages" can be seen to come straight from the deepest, most profound part of the self which religious people believe is the "kingdom of God".

We are told in the gospel that when Pontius Pilate was judging Jesus, his wife sent a message to him saying that she had dreamed about Jesus, and begging her husband to "have nothing to do with this just man". Now maybe this was not a message from whatever God Pilate's wife believed in, but from deep within her. Maybe Pilate's wife knew about Jesus, perhaps through servants. Maybe she thought about him, wondered about him, thought he was probably a good man and worried about her husband's involvement. She was the wife of a Roman governor however, and it was probably difficult if not impossible to discuss it. Because of this, her great anxiety expressed itself in a dream, a deep wish that her husband, Pilate should not be responsible for his death.

The same goes for the dream of Joseph, that he should marry Mary. Mary was expecting a baby, and was not officially living with Joseph. This was bad but deep within himself in his feelings, he knew that Mary was a good woman, and he loved her. His anxiety and desire was resolved in his dream, telling him simply to marry her. Strangely we are never told, in the books about Jesus, that Joseph loved Mary. Too dangerous of course, this marriage had to be emotionless and celibate. For the Church, Mary and Joseph were dedicated to God, not to each other.

But - can anyone imagine growing up in a family where the parents do not love one another? Only too easily, many have experienced it and we see examples in the soaps on our TV every evening. It is simply hell, because the child assumes that this lack of love is his fault. The Catholic Church insists that Jesus was an only child. Only children especially, are subjected to every nuance of feelings in a family, for there are no others to share these feelings with. Jesus could never have grown up loving everyone he knew, and wanting to love the whole world, without having parents who loved one another deeply.

The dream of St. Peter in which he was told to eat "unclean food", representing the gentiles, goes to show the depth of his devotion to the Jewish traditions in which he had been raised. His entire upbringing as a traditional Jew told him that nothing unclean, whether food or human beings should be admitted to the community of God. But, Peter knew that this was the *exact opposite of what Jesus had taught; love and acceptance for all men.* Because of this splitting, this conflict within himself, Peter's conscious mind could not solve the problem, but his unconscious mind, as a result of his years with Jesus, resolved the problem for him in a dream or vision.

"What God has called clean, you must not call unclean." Acts.

It is said that scientists, mathematicians and inventors often have dreams which present the solution to some problem over which they have been worrying. In fact all of these dreams would then come within the Freudian definition of a dream as representing a powerful desire. These dreams, visions, desires, are important. They come from the depth of the soul and often provide solutions which the dreamer cannot solve by reason alone, it needs the depth of imagination and desire, set free in dreams.

This way of looking at dreams as representing the deepest desires of the dreamer, can only strengthen the sense of the worth of a human being, and the miracle of the human spirit. Instead of making knee-jerk responses to external messages manifested in rather strange ways, these people in the Bible are acting from the deepest yearning and understanding of their own souls. The unconscious is wiser than the conscious mind, knowing only the truth of the dreamer's feelings, in ways in which the conscious mind often does not.

This would explain other dreams, which seem less hopeful. It is said that some great saint once had a vision of Hell, and that he saw a vast number of human souls, falling down there, like leaves falling from the trees in autumn. If we work on this dream in the way we have looked at others, we can simply say that this was a terror deep within the man, in his inmost self. It may not have been about hell at all, but his own sense of being lost and destroyed in the utmost pain. So great was his anxiety, that it was manifested as a dream.

This stops us from looking at this dream as a fact, revealed by God, and places it firmly in the pathology of the man who had the dream. One could no doubt analyse this, if one knew much of his background. For some reason he had a terror of hell, probably the hell of his childhood, which emerged in his sleep.

VISION

Dreams and visions are personal, but we must not lose the idea of Vision.

All great saints had vision. For many of them these came to them visually while they were awake, and we then say they had visions. Think of the great visions of the Old Testament.

At the time of Ezekiel, the whole of the Jewish people was sent to Babylon and the end of the Jewish people seemed certain. In the same way as for Jews in the concentration camps, it seemed that God had finally deserted his people. Ezekiel believed with all his might that God was still with his people, that it was not the end, that there was still hope. He was sure, deep down, that God was not left behind in the temple at Jerusalem, but had travelled with his people to be with them in their suffering.

Ezekiel experienced this conviction as a great vision or dream. He told of great visions of God, the Ancient of Days, transported in a mighty chariot from Jerusalem to Babylon. God was still with them. He also saw a whole dry valley of bones, and skeletons. Suddenly a great wind began to blow, the spirit of God was upon his people, and the skeletons were clothed with flesh and rose up, living, vibrant human beings, restored by God.

Israel had been destroyed, but Ezekiel had the deep conviction that it would rise again. By means of these visions he was able to rally the Jews until eventually the day came when thousands of them did actually return to Israel and began to rebuild the temple. Ezekiel's visions had huge political and practical repercussions.

The same thing can be said about Martin Luther King, whose cry "I have a Dream" and his vision of little black children and little white children living and playing together, resonated across the world.

What is important here is the power, wonder and value of the human imagination, which is linked to our deepest desires and yearnings. Desires are not only for sex and for food, but also, in Ezekiel's case, for the survival of a whole race. Dreams and visions have the same origin, the yearning and powerful convictions of the unconscious mind.

Pope John XXIII, an elderly man in his eighties, had vision. He had a vision of a great council of the Church. After two terrible world wars, the destruction of the cities and populations of Europe by bombs and gunfire, the death of millions in the Nazi death camps and the frozen wastes of Russia, the destruction of great cities and the death of thousands in

Japan from the atom bomb, this great Council would discuss all the great questions of the Church and the world,

Horrified at the thought of the enormous amount of time, money and organisation needed, and overwhelmed by the thought of all the preparation, a cardinal desperately asked him *why* he needed a Church Council. Pope John gave no detailed reasons, instead he answered with an image - he threw open one of the windows in the room, and said simply,

"To let in some fresh air."

This was the greatest vision of the Church in the twentieth century. It had breadth, love, compassion, understanding, equality of men and women and openness to the world.

In fact to many of us, men in the Vatican seem to have been back-pedalling from the Second Vatican Council as fast as they can. In the same way that Barak Obama is being vilified by those who hate his vision, there are powerful people in the Church who, because of their own problems, hate Vatican II with their whole being and are doing their level best to make sure that the reforms it advocated do not happen.

These people have been busy slamming all the windows shut ever since Pope John opened them. They are terrified of the vision, which it presented. They know full well that if the real vision of Vatican II is ever implemented wholeheartedly across the Church, their control will be destroyed and their own mental balance depends on their control..

They cannot bear vision: they want control. Why do they so desperately need to control? Because of their early lives, their childhoods, the only way that they can hold themselves together is by rigid control, and that means controlling others. This is a psychological problem, not a spiritual one. The trouble is that some of them have power in the Church which most of us do not.

The terrified person, the paranoid person, is afraid of draughts. Everything is seen as a threat. Open windows frighten them. In her great book, *Emma,* Jane Austen describes Mr. Woodhouse, an elderly timid man, who is terrified of change of any kind. Unable to prevent the young people from organising a dance, he complains at length about draughts and the danger they present to bodies heated by dancing. He begs them not to open any windows. There are many people in the Church who are like Mr. Woodhouse. They don't like fresh air, they are afraid of draughts.

The particular vision of the Church which some Catholic priests had in Latin America, and called "liberation theology", is regarded with horror by many in the Church, because it means a loosening of traditional Catholicism.

Why are people afraid of their dreams and vision? Because of their own childhood development, people have a defensive need for self-control,/ They are afraid of their own imaginations, afraid of what is deeply buried within them. Also, if you are convinced that religion is totally rational and intellectual, dreams and visions cannot fit into this scenario, because they are not rational at all, but may reveal a deeper human wisdom. Imagination and reason balance one another out. The imagination projects a goal, but logic may show how to go about it.

Whatever you think about the reality of the Resurrection, it is the greatest imaginative doctrine of all time. A Man who was killed as a criminal two thousand years ago still lives in the millions of hearts, minds, souls and bodies, of those who believe in Him.

Our dreams and visions often seem crazy, they seem totally at odds with the rational world. But this is because people are not totally rational

- we are creatures of imagination, symbols, impulse and creativity. Our highest achievements are not only physical but also imaginative and creative. We express ourselves in music, stories, pictures, poetry and drama.

When man reached the moon, it was not only an enormous technological achievement; it answered to the height of the imagination of mankind. "Do you want the moon to play with?" went a lullaby of my childhood, and the crazy answer is, "Yes, we do."

Imagination is one of the greatest gifts and an extraordinary result of evolution. Does imagination help us to survive in the human jungle? Of course it does. We flock to those with a dream or a mission, Martin Luther King, Desmond Tutu, Gandhi, Mother Theresa, Pope John XXIII, the present Pope Francis, saints like Francis, or Mother Julian of Norwich, musicians like Bach, Bernstein, Lloyd Weber, artists and poets. Without vision we die.

The imagination is an extraordinary thing because we can imagine situations totally different to the one that we are in. Against all the evidence to the contrary, we can imagine and hope for a world full of love, joy, creativity, compassion, and freedom from fear, cruelty, anxiety and poverty.

In ancient times, men flocked to the great heroes, like Alexander the Great, who dreamed of conquering a world. He did conquer a world, and brought destruction and death to thousands, including many of his own. The Christian does not have a warrior hero; he has Jesus, who told of love instead of hatred, respect and compassion instead of indifference, equality instead of power and forgiveness instead of revenge. Freud was not a Christian, but a man of deep imagination, who thought that by listening to people, and helping them to love others, it would be possible to help rid mankind of some of its inner demons.

This is what it means to be a Catholic, a Christian, and at heart, Jewish or Muslim too. In spite of all the wars, the cruelty, the hatred, the paranoia, the greed, the rage, the starvation, poverty and suffering; we can all imagine, and we can keep trying to create, something infinitely better. Because we can imagine it, because our religion holds out the hope of a world full of hope, faith, trust and love, we feel we can all do something, however small, to bring it about.

Christianity, contrary to the ideas of those who would nail it down to a rigid cross with nails of iron, is deeply imaginative, creative, and sublime. To try and confine the whole of religious experience within the narrow confines of a catechism is doomed to failure, for this is not what it is about.

There is a story of a great theologian, a saint, who was trying to understand the mysteries of God. Walking upon the seashore, lost in thought, struggling with the mystery, he saw a small boy playing. The boy had dug a hole and was running back and forward to the sea with a spoon. Amused, the saint asked the little boy what he was doing. The child answered that he was trying to fill the hole with sea water, but as soon as he dropped in a spoon of water, it disappeared into the sand at the bottom of the hole. Kindly, the saint explained that this was an impossible task, and that no matter how much he tried; the hole would never fill with sea water. The child straightened up, and looking the wise man in the eye, he said,

"No more can you understand the mysteries of God, with your human mind."

In other words, God can be *experienced* but not intellectually understood. We do not need to know *about* God, we need to *experience* God. It does not matter whether the above story is true or not, we can experience it in our hearts. There is a great power in the universe called Love, which cannot be pinned down as a rational concept, except maybe, "We all hang together, or we all hang separately."

Chapter Sixteen

The Meeting

That we may all meet merrily in Heaven.

St. Thomas More.

Heaven, like the universe, is infinite in dimensions and variety. There are parts of Heaven that have yet to be discovered, quiet backwaters where you can escape the crowds, the harps and the choirs and relax with a cup of coffee. So it happened that on a quiet sunny morning, Jesus found himself as usual in Heaven, but outside a café.

Seated at a table, in the warm sunshine, was a small dark haired man, wearing a good three-piece suit, with a neatly trimmed beard and moustache and a large cigar clamped firmly between his teeth. His legs were stretched out before him and he had an air of contentment.

"Still smoking I see," observed Jesus, as he sat down opposite.

"Can't do me any harm now," said Freud, for it was he. "Been there, done that, died from cancer, and, as they keep saying around here, 'got the tee shirt'." He peered at the Man opposite.

"You're supposed to know everything," he said, "What is a tee shirt?"

Jesus looked vague, "Not sure," he said, "I think it's a sort of short tunic with writing on it."

"Ah," said the other, "fashion eh?" And they both nodded reflectively.

At this point a hovering angel, who was wearing black trousers and a white shirt to preserve the atmosphere, placed a large cappuccino with chocolate before each man, for there are no joys which cannot be found in Heaven. As they sipped in the warm sun, Freud suddenly frowned.

"It's no use trying to convert me," he said, "it's too late. Besides, I'm an unbelieving Jew. You know that."

"I'm Jewish myself," observed his companion, "in case you hadn't noticed. And the High Priest wasn't too keen on me either. He said I was a blasphemer."

They smiled wryly.

Freud became thoughtful. "Did you hear about that murderous gentile called Hitler? In Austria too. My own sisters died in the gas chambers! They tried to wipe us out!   He rocked, grieving, for a while.

"Yes", said Jesus soberly after a while. "They didn't succeed though. We're still around."

"What happened to him?" asked Freud.

"Still working on it," said Jesus, "It was a bad case; takes time."

Freud nodded sagely, "I had cases which took years," he said. He looked sideways at Jesus. "Bad case of sexual repression, I suppose?" he said.

"Repression, right," was the reply. "Not sexual though, that was a symptom. The real problem was incredible, intolerable, unbearable pain.

He repressed it, then he had to inflict it on others you see. Made him feel better."

"Trauma theory!" snorted Freud. "Trauma theory! It was repressed sexuality, I tell you. You're beginning to sound like Jung. I thought you would know better!"

"You believed in Trauma Theory yourself, at one time," said Jesus mildly, "Before it became too difficult to hold on to. In fact you discovered it."

Freud puffed on his cigar angrily and then sighed.

"Even Jung was right about some things," said Jesus, "and even you couldn't be right about everything. Those women really were traumatised, you know. They really had suffered abominably at the hands of the men who were supposed to be looking after them. You did brilliantly though, you listened to them. You took them seriously; no one had ever done that before. You made people realise that there was more to being human than intellect and will-power."

Jesus smiled. "Not that you don't have a brilliant intellect," he added diplomatically. "But you got them to talk, you listened, no one else did that. And even more important, you spent your life trying to understand."

Freud nodded and relaxed. "I'm a city man," he said complacently. "Vienna was the greatest cultural city of Europe. There are advantages to being a city man - present company excepted," he added. "There is something in the atmosphere of a city, the friends, the ideas, the buzz, the meetings, the excitement, the arguments, the cut and thrust. It makes for curiosity, for a search for truth. Nazareth was all very well, but it wasn't a place for the cutting edge of intellectual thought, was it?"

"Can anything good come out of Nazareth?" Jesus asked ruefully. "You remind me of my friend Paul. Now there was a city man, if ever I knew one. Always full of ideas was Paul."

"Someone talking about me?"

Another short dark man with a neatly trimmed beard and moustache came across the plaza, and Paul, for he it was, sat between the other two. Another cappuccino appeared.

"Someone talking about me?" he asked again with a beaming smile.

"We were talking about Jews," said Jesus.

"Right! Right!" said Paul, for in Heaven everyone turns up at the right moment. "That's me all right. I was an observant Jew. I kept the law. I worshipped in the temple, I made the sacrifices, and I observed the Sabbath. But since you came" he nodded to Jesus, "everything has changed. But.... I always said, I always said.... you know I did.... that this good news about Universal Love wasn't just for us. It was for everyone! We must tell the Greeks and the Romans," I said. "This is for everyone."

A fist banged down on the table.

"My point exactly," chimed in Freud eagerly. "I always said, this idea of understanding the unconscious, in order to heal people, must not be kept among Jews. We have discovered it, but the poets knew it first, and it is for the whole world! That was why I insisted that Jung, a Christian, should be made President of the Psychoanalytical Association. We needed people who were not Jews to spread the word. They could dismiss us as Jews. But this applies to the whole of mankind."

"Right again!" cried Paul. "I took the message of love to the Gentiles. I went to Greece, to Athens itself. Athens! But they could not believe," he mourned, "even though they had an altar to the Unknown God. I thought that might appeal to them."

"Athens?" echoed Freud. "How could they? They were past the age of myths and poetry by then, hooked on the logic and reason of their philosophers, Plato, Aristotle. By that time everything with them was intellect, reason, will power and control of the passions, or feelings. How could they understand the over-riding power of the unconscious? Neither," he added, looking at Jesus, "could you."

"Me?" cried Jesus. "Did I not say that it is not what goes into a man which defiles him, but what comes out of him? Lies and evil words and thoughts! You were not the only one to cure mad men. I found one naked in a harsh valley of rocks, beneath the burning sun, crying aloud and cutting himself with stones. A short time later he was sitting quiet, clothed and in his right mind. He wanted to stay with me, but I would not let him."

"Quite right," said Freud. "They always want to stay forever, but if they are really cured," he added earnestly, "they must go out into the world. But that man sounds psychotic, quite crazy, the sort of person Jung used to deal with."

A large man with spectacles approached them. Another chair appeared.

"The crazy?" asked Jung. "Really crazy?" I used to listen to them for hours. "There is more in their insanity, I always said, than in the sanity of others."

"You said a lot of other things too," said Freud stiffly. "You would have done better to keep your mouth shut."

"Always the Father, always the Authority!" answered Jung angrily. "You could not forgive me for being different!"

"Gentlemen! Gentlemen!" It was Paul who cried out. "Remember where you are. Fatherhood is different here. Does it matter which of you is the greatest? I had disciples crying, 'I am for Peter,' or 'I am for Paul,' but we are all for God and for one another. We are for humanity. Cries of 'I am for Jung' or 'I am for Freud' make no sense here."

There was a tense silence, which was broken by Jesus calling for more cappuccino. The angel, who recognised a crisis when he saw it, hurriedly placed the steaming cups on the table, together with a plate of very fancy biscuits.

"Well," said Freud broodingly, "it was a long time ago."

"An eternity," said Jesus. "Those days are gone. There is no more mourning or weeping."

"But that was the problem," cried Freud. "So much mourning, and weeping, so much hidden grief, so much hidden sorrow, so much unknown suffering. So many feelings repressed, deep down, where they could not know about them. Is it a wonder than men often seemed to be insane?"

"And were insane," added Jung. "Their sufferings had driven them mad." He frowned for a while, then smiled suddenly.

"Do you remember," he asked Freud, "how when we first met, we talked and talked for seventeen hours without a break? Your wife thought we had gone crazy!"

"We were crazy," said Freud, "crazy with joy. We understood one another. I had not met anyone who understood me so thoroughly."

He and Jung cleared their throats and looked self-conscious for a while, then relaxed cautiously.

At this point, a rather large monk who seemed a bit pre-occupied and absent-minded rambled up to them. He wore a white religious habit, with a long black tabard.

"Thomas Aquinas!" cried Jesus. "My faithful preacher. Come and join us."

"I have been listening," said Thomas. "You did not see me, but I was listening. There is so much to understand. I tried to find the truth, but they used my words in order to persecute others." He turned to Jesus.

"You," he said, "You were the Truth, the Way and the Life. But they could not believe that Truth was Love, and a Suffering Man. Neither did I then. I wanted precision, arguments, intellectual statements, explicit, organised formulas based on what I thought was reason. I rejoiced in reason, I bathed in it and thought it was the answer to everything. I was wrong. Before I died, I said that everything I had written was as straw, I told them, because I had a vision of the Mystery of Love to which we were called, and the enormous compassion and forgiveness."

"We have been set free from the wisdom of men," said Paul gently. "It is time for the wisdom of God."

"*Now*, I see," said the monk, "But I wanted philosophy. Everyone was going crazy about philosophy. It was the wisdom of the time you see. The Greek books had finally reached us from Constantinople – Aristotle and Plato! Can you imagine? After all those centuries! After hundreds of years of fighting, constant wars, illiteracy and barbarity, we finally seemed to have order and a rational society within our grasp. We had universities! After eight hundred years we had universities all over Christendom!

At that time every nobleman was trained to be a warrior – often even the bishops and the Pope himself. After all that violent insanity, I wanted to create an orderly peaceful society. I wanted that on earth, it should be as it is in Heaven, but I chose the wrong means."

"Maybe it was necessary at the time," said Paul.

"I know," said Thomas, "But before I died, I understood, and I tried to tell them. But it was too late. They wanted absolute certainty, formulas that could be pinned down, intellectual statements that could admit no error. Arguments that could send a man to the fire, or Hell itself, if he could not agree with them."

Freud stretched his legs, put his hands in his pockets and began to speak. He felt on very firm ground.

"They had suffered enormous repression," he said. "Remember the circumstances in which they lived. Everyone crowded together in small spaces. No one had privacy. Sex and violence were rampant parents were harsh. They were split, narcissistic. They wanted to be good, but they were haunted by the terrible visions in their dreams, with no means of understanding them. No-one did," and he looked modest, "until I wrote my book about Dreams."

"Dreams", he went on, "are the Royal Highroad to the Unconscious. That is how we find out what is in a man or woman. What were the dreams of Joan of Arc, with her saints and her visions? She was a good girl, a daughter of the Church, but she could fight like a man, and loathed the war and harassment to which her country was subjected. She was a greater general and strategist than any of the others. It was her dreams and visions that told her so. But no-one understood in her day. If she had used reason, no one would have taken any notice, it was too soon, so she had dreams and visions"

Jung broke in. "Many of them were insane," he said. "The spiritual world kept breaking through and often it was demonic."

"Absolute rubbish!" an angry woman was among them now. "The demons were in their heads. They had been tormented, tortured, often by fathers, or guardians. Sexual play and abuse were common. They had to block out the suffering, they split off any compassion they might have had. They could only act out the violence, because they could not remember their own suffering, and so they tormented others in order to obtain relief. Their nightmares were not from external demons but from the incredible torments of their own minds. There is a man," she added reflectively, "Lloyd de Mause, and he says that all children in the past were what we would call abused."

"Alice Miller!" said Jesus greeting her. He turned to her. "The abuse went far deeper than people like to think. Think of the children in my day, in every country where the Romans held sway. Seeing men slaughtered in the "games", men crucified in public and people gathered around to watch. At Rome they crucified two thousand slaves! Two thousand men dying slowly on stakes at the roadside. The children were brutalized".

"Exactly," said Alice. "Could the children see that and not develop their own powerful defences against suffering? Perhaps it was their father or brother dying slowly in agony. The younger ones forgot it, they had too in order to survive, repress the terror, and that made them forget that men could suffer, and made them harsh and uncaring."

"They became totally cut off from their own feelings," said Freud. "It was bound to happen. Their repressed their feelings of pain and then went on to inflict pain on others."

"You! You can talk." cried Alice. "You ignored the women who told you of sexual abuse when it became too much for you. You invented the Oedipus complex to cover up your mistake."

"I was wrong," said Freud. "I see that now. But how difficult was it to believe at that time that grave, respectable men, important men, were sexually abusing their daughters? And anyway," he added, "Say what you like. The Oedipus complex is an important theory. It was not wasted time. It was important, and still is."

"Excuse me," Another priest, but this time wearing a mitre on his head. "I am Augustine. I was there when the Roman Empire collapsed. The barbarians were pouring across Europe, and then from Spain to North Africa. They brought darkness and chaos, government by fierce, illiterate warriors instead of philosophers. I did my best to stem the tide. The barbarians were there, swarming, at the gates of Hippo, my city, as I lay dying. I knew there was neither hope nor help. There were thousands of them, raging and screaming for blood and gold. They burned the libraries. There was no help from Rome, Things were collapsing over there too; there was no civilized place to escape to."

Alice Miller looked even more fierce. "Years before, when there was no crisis, you sent your wife back to Africa by herself though," she said, "just because your mother wanted you to! Maybe Freud was right about the Oedipus complex," she added thoughtfully.

"She was not my wife," said Augustine stiffly, "She was my sinful concubine. May God forgive me for my weakness of the flesh. But I overcame my evil desires in the end, and sent her back."

"She was only your concubine because you wouldn't marry her," raged Alice. "She lived with you, looked after you, waited for you for many years and bore your child. But you hated all women, except your mother, and thought they were evil, so you had to send her back to save your precious virtue. Virtue! You kept the boy though. Lloyd de Mause was right about children being abused in most of history. You thought nothing of tearing a boy away from his mother, never to see her again, in order to save your precious virtue! You wanted him to be a spiritual and beautiful mirror image of yourself, but he died young. Probably of grief at being ripped away from his mother, I wouldn't wonder."

There was a general stirring and clearing of masculine throats at this point. Augustine looked unhappy. He gazed long at Jesus, and then slowly removed his mitre.

"It has no use here," he said. "There is no-one here who needs re-minding of what I was. I did wrong, I see that. But I did not know. I wanted to hold up the City of God, but I also wanted to salvage what I could of the Empire of Rome. Rome was all that we knew, the centre of civilisation. "I wanted to raise up a Spiritual Rome based on the love of God, to take the place of the Old Order."

"There was still Constantinople," said Jung thoughtfully.

"No" said Augustine. "Terrible things happened there too. But without Rome it was only a matter of time before Constantinople fell too, and then all would be dark."

"Rome did survive though," said Thomas Aquinas, "and Benedict kept the monasteries going. He kept the libraries, the book copying, he kept the tradition of learning, and he taught the young. But like everything else, success brings envy. The wealthy and powerful sent their own sons to run the monasteries and the surrounding lands, and so the monasteries became political pawns, and the bishops too," he added. "Eventually the great kings tried to use their own sons as bishops to run the church as political support for their own power games."

There was suddenly a chuckle, a woman was laughing and there stood a small elderly nun swathed in black. She looked very cheerful.

"Why, my Lords," she said, "They were terrible times indeed and there was so much suffering and grief. Yet in a vision my Lord came to me, his simple servant, Julian of Norwich, and he told me that sin is No Thing. He showed me this." She held out her hand, and there in the palm of her hand was a small hazel nut. "He showed me this," she repeated, happily, "And he told me to look well, for small though it is, it is the whole universe, and I am to remember three things, He created it, He cares for it, and He loves it. He told me to remember that - All shall be Well, All shall be Well, and All manner of things shall be Well."

Suddenly everything seemed to have changed. They were no longer in a café on the pavement of Heaven; they were in a twentieth century room, which had carpet on the floor and curtains at the windows. It had a large desk, books everywhere, and many small statues of ancient gods and goddesses, Greek, Roman and Egyptian. Along one wall was a large couch, which was covered with cushions and coloured rugs. It was Freud's consulting room.

"My old room!" cried Freud in glee. "My old room! I left it behind when I escaped the Nazis and went to England. I tried to create something like it in Hampstead. I never thought to see it again."

He wandered around, picking up papers, books and pens putting them down again, and then picking up small statuettes.

"Lord!" exclaimed Augustine in horror. "These are pagan gods. They are Idols. Permit me to destroy and burn them now."

"Just like the Sons of Thunder," observed Jesus. "There is always someone who wishes to destroy. He who is not against you is for you."

"I am against you," cried Freud. "I always have been. You know that."

"You were for mankind," said Jesus. "Am I not a man? You heard their suffering and their cries for help. You tried to understand. Not many people tried to help as you did."

"Even if you got it wrong," interrupted Alice fiercely.

Jesus went on, "Some of those who believed themselves to be good Christians and Catholics treated men, women and children cruelly and dismissively."

At this point the group broke up. Freud and Paul seemed to have a great deal in common and were talking earnestly. Others drifted into groups, all serious and argumentative. More food and drink appeared and the nineteenth century men lit cigars. Jesus looked around in a satisfied sort of way, congratulated the angel on his success and wandered outside.

He was now in a large kitchen, opening onto a garden. There were many women and children here. Some of them looked enquiringly at the room Jesus came from. He smiled at them, and a group of women drifted off to join in the discussions.

"Still arguing, are they?" asked a woman who had been bustling around, pushing the attendant angels out of the way as she did so.

"Still arguing Martha," said Jesus, "but at least they *are* arguing and not shouting at one another."

"Typical," said another woman. "The men go on arguing while we go on feeding the kids, cleaning the house and preparing the meals."

"Then they have the nerve to tell us what to do and how to do it," chimed in another.

"Why don't you tell them how it is?" asked Jesus. "Everyone is equal here, there is no more male and female, no more Jew and Gentile, as Paul said."

"They don't listen," said one of the women, and there was a murmur of agreement.

"Look at the men in there. Some of them have been running the Church for centuries. When it was powerful, they were right in there. Now the church is weak, many of them don't know what to do. They still think it is about power and authority."

"The church has been a men's club for centuries, even if women were the more faithful church-goers," said another. "They invite women to go to their meetings, but it is one, or maybe two women, the ones they think are worthy. They choose the ones who are often like them, or agree with them."

"They tried that with the psychoanalytic movement also," said another, totally different woman, in rather elegant twentieth century clothes and a hat. "We were not having that. We moved in. Besides, the women analysts were often more sensitive than the men. Some of us were trained medically as they were, so they could not really keep us out. Freud, whom I follow absolutely in everything, nevertheless did not understand the role of the mother. It was I, Melanie Klein, who drew their attention to the needs and sufferings of the baby."

The women now began to talk among themselves, as the men were. Some more of them drifted off into the discussion room with the men. The ones left kept an eye on the children, but it was only out of habit, for after all this was Heaven and nothing could go wrong.

Jesus noted that everything seemed to be going satisfactorily. He went slowly out of the door, across the garden, and walked out onto a beach, where the waves were lapping the sand, and the sun was shining, with a gentle breeze. He saw some men by fishing boats, mending their nets, and smiled at happy memories. Some of the children were playing there. As so often on earth, he began walking along the seashore. After a little while, he was joined by Freud, and they walked along together, deep in discussion.

Bibliography

The New Testament

Attachment.   John Bowlby

Separation – Anxiety and Anger   John Bowlby

The Psychopathology of Everyday Life   Sigmund Freud

Why Love Matters: Sue Gerhardt.

The God of Surprises   Gerard Hughes

Revelations of Divine Love   Julian of Norwich

The History of Childhood Edited by Lloyd de   Mause

The medium is the Message   Marshall McLuhan

The Drama of Being a Child   Alice Miller

For Your Own Good   Alice Miller

The Body Never Lies   Alice Miller

Eunuchs for the Kingdom of Heaven   Uta Ranke-
                                                     Heineman

Cries Unheard, the Story of Mary Bell   Gita Sereny

The god of the Left Hemisphere   Roderick Tweedy

Boarding School Syndrome   Joy Shaverien

The Future of Man   Teilhard de
                                                     Chardin

The penny Catechism

◆ ◆ ◆

Proof of Heaven   Eben Alexander
(Not a proof at all, but a different approach to consciousness).

Made in the USA
Charleston, SC
21 December 2015